Social Studies

myWorld INTERACTIVE

2

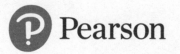 Pearson

Boston, Massachusetts   Chandler, Arizona
Glenview, Illinois   New York, New York

Pearson would like to extend a special thank you to all of the teachers who helped guide the development of this program. We gratefully acknowledge your efforts to realize the possibilities of elementary Social Studies teaching and learning. Together, we will prepare students for college, careers, and civic life.

Cover: Andy Sacks/Getty Images

Credits appear on pages R30–R31, which constitute an extension of this copyright page.

ISBN-13: 978-0-328-97309-5
ISBN-10: 0-328-97309-2

3 18

Program Authors

Dr. Linda B. Bennett
Faculty, Social Studies Education
College of Education
University of Missouri
Columbia, MO

Dr. James B. Kracht
Professor Emeritus
Departments of Geography and
  Teaching, Learning, and Culture
Texas A&M University
College Station, TX

Reviewers and Consultants

Program Consultants

ELL Consultant
Jim Cummins Ph.D.

Professor Emeritus,
Department of
  Curriculum, Teaching,
  and Learning
University of Toronto
Toronto, Canada

Differentiated Instruction
Consultant

Kathy Tuchman Glass
President of Glass
  Educational Consulting
Woodside, CA

Reading Consultant
Elfrieda H. Hiebert Ph.D.

Founder, President and
  CEO, TextProject, Inc.
University of California
  Santa Cruz

Inquiry and C3 Consultant

Dr. Kathy Swan
Professor of Curriculum
  and Instruction
University of Kentucky
Lexington, KY

Academic Reviewers

Paul Apodaca, Ph.D.

Associate Professor,
  American Studies
Chapman University
Orange, CA

Warren J. Blumenfeld, Ed.D.

Former Associate
  Professor, Iowa State
  University, School
  of Education
South Hadley, MA

Dr. Albert M. Camarillo

Professor of History,
  Emeritus
Stanford University
Palo Alto, CA

Dr. Shirley A. James Hanshaw

Professor, Department
  of English
Mississippi State
  University
Mississippi State, MS

Xiaojian Zhao

Professor, Department
  of Asian American
  Studies
University of California,
  Santa Barbara
Santa Barbara, CA

Teacher Reviewers

Mercedes Kirk
First grade teacher
Folsom Cordova USD
Folsom, CA

Julie Martire
Teacher, Grade 5
Flocktown Elementary School
Long Valley, NJ

Kristy H. Spears
K-5 Reading Specialist
Pleasant Knoll Elementary School
Fort Mill, SC

Kristin Sullens
Teacher, Grade 4
Chula Vista ESD
San Diego, CA

Program Partner

Campaign for the Civic Mission of Schools is a coalition of
over 70 national civic learning, education, civic engagement,
and business groups committed to improving the quality and
quantity of civic learning in American schools.

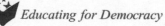

Campaign for the Civic Mission of Schools
Educating for Democracy

🌐 Map and Graph Skills Handbook

✏️ Writing Workshop

🔍 Using Primary and Secondary Sources

Families Today and In the Past

GO ONLINE FOR DIGITAL RESOURCES

📖 eTEXT

▶ VIDEO

Big Question Video
How Does Life Change Throughout History?

🔊 AUDIO

Sing About It! lyrics and music

👆 INTERACTIVITY

- **Big Question Activity**
  How Does Life Change Throughout History?
- **Quest Interactivities**
  Quest Kick Off, Quest Connections, Quest Findings
- **Lesson Interactivities**
  Lesson Introduction, Lesson Review
- **Digital Skill Practice**
  Sequence, Interpret Timelines

🎮 GAMES

Vocabulary Practice

☑ ASSESSMENT

Lesson Quizzes and Chapter Tests

The BIG Question How does life change throughout history?

Chapter 2
People, Places, and Nature

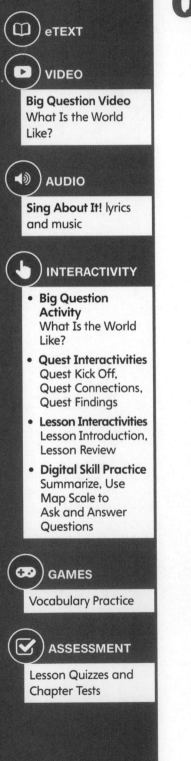

GO ONLINE FOR
DIGITAL RESOURCES

📖 eTEXT

▶ VIDEO

Big Question Video
What Is the World
Like?

🔊 AUDIO

Sing About It! lyrics
and music

👆 INTERACTIVITY

• **Big Question
  Activity**
  What Is the World
  Like?
• **Quest Interactivities**
  Quest Kick Off,
  Quest Connections,
  Quest Findings
• **Lesson Interactivities**
  Lesson Introduction,
  Lesson Review
• **Digital Skill Practice**
  Summarize, Use
  Map Scale to
  Ask and Answer
  Questions

🎮 GAMES

Vocabulary Practice

☑ ASSESSMENT

Lesson Quizzes and
Chapter Tests

The BIG Question What is the world like?

GO ONLINE FOR DIGITAL RESOURCES

📖 eTEXT

▶ VIDEO

Big Question Video
How Does Government Work?

🔊 AUDIO

Sing About It! lyrics and music

👆 INTERACTIVITY

- **Big Question Activity** How Does Government Work?
- **Quest Interactivities** Quest Kick Off, Quest Connections, Quest Findings
- **Lesson Interactivities** Lesson Introduction, Lesson Review
- **Digital Skill Practice** Cause and Effect, Solve a Problem

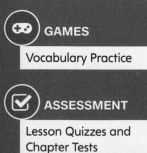 GAMES

Vocabulary Practice

☑ ASSESSMENT

Lesson Quizzes and Chapter Tests

The BIG Question How does government work?

Chapter 4

People Who Supply Our Goods and Services

GO ONLINE FOR DIGITAL RESOURCES

📖 eTEXT

▶ VIDEO

Big Question Video
How Do People Get What They Need?

🔊 AUDIO

Sing About It! lyrics and music

👆 INTERACTIVITY

- **Big Question Activity**
  How Do People Get What They Need?
- **Quest Interactivities**
  Quest Kick Off, Quest Connections, Quest Findings
- **Lesson Interactivities**
  Lesson Introduction, Lesson Review
- **Digital Skill Practice**
  Identify Main Idea and Details, Analyze Costs and Benefits

🎮 GAMES

Vocabulary Practice

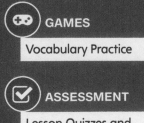

✅ ASSESSMENT

Lesson Quizzes and Chapter Tests

The BIG Question How do people get what they need?

Chapter 5 — Making a Difference

GO ONLINE FOR DIGITAL RESOURCES

📖 eTEXT

▶ VIDEO

Big Question Video
What Makes Someone a Hero?

🔊 AUDIO

Sing About It! lyrics and music

👆 INTERACTIVITY

- **Big Question Activity**
  What Makes Someone a Hero?
- **Quest Interactivities**
  Quest Kick Off,
  Quest Connections,
  Quest Findings
- **Lesson Interactivities**
  Lesson Introduction,
  Lesson Review
- **Digital Skill Practice**
  Compare and Contrast, Analyze Images

🎮 GAMES

Vocabulary Practice

☑ ASSESSMENT

Lesson Quizzes and Chapter Tests

The BIG Question — What makes someone a hero?

Our American Culture

The **BIG** Question **How is culture shared?**

Quests

Ask questions, explore sources, and cite evidence to support your view!

Maps

Where did this happen? Find out on these maps in your text.

Maps continued

Graphs and Charts

Find these charts, graphs, and tables in your text. They'll help you pull it together.

Primary Sources

Read primary sources to hear voices from the time.

People to Know

Read about the people who made history.

Citizenship

Biographies Online

Bella Abzug

Abigail Adams

Jane Addams

Susan B. Anthony

Clara Barton

Chaz Bono

Daniel Boone

Ruby Bridges

Juan Rodriguez Cabrillo

George Washington Carver

César Chávez

Sophie Cubbison

Marie Sklodowska Curie

Charles Drew

Henri Dunant

Thomas Edison

Albert Einstein

Benjamin Franklin

Betty Friedan

Dolores Huerta

Billie Jean King

Martin Luther King, Jr.

Yuri Kochiyama

Abraham Lincoln

Iqbal Masih

Golda Meir

Harvey Milk

José Montoya

John Muir

Gavin Newsom

Florence Nightingale

Rosa Parks

Louis Pasteur

Pocahontas

Sally Ride

Jackie Robinson

Eleanor Roosevelt

Wilma Rudolph

Jonas Salk

José Julio Sarria

George Shima

Sitting Bull

Gloria Steinem

Harriet Tubman

Booker T. Washington

George Washington

Malala Yousafzai

This book will give you a lot of chances to figure things out. Then you can show what you have figured out and give your reasons.

The Quest Kick Off will tell you the goal of the Quest.

You can get started right away.

Watch for Quest Connections all through the chapter.

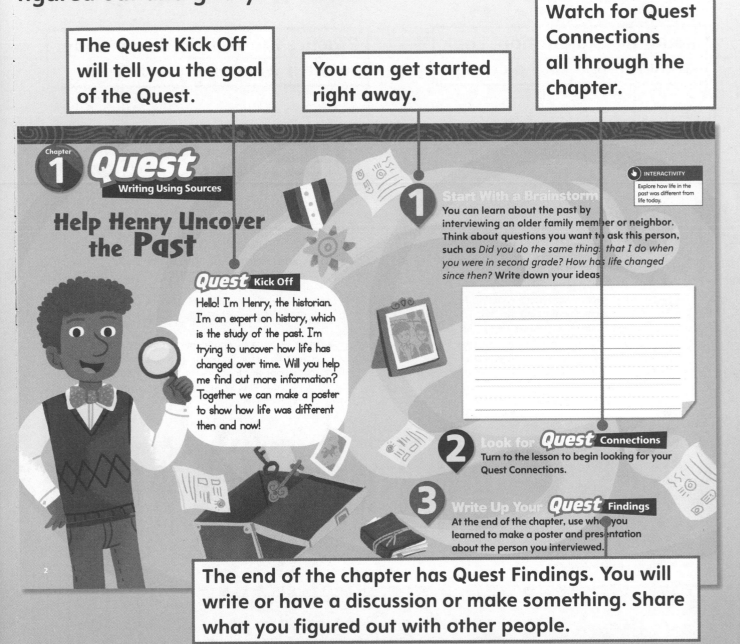

The end of the chapter has Quest Findings. You will write or have a discussion or make something. Share what you figured out with other people.

2. Find two words with yellow highlight. What are they?

3. Find another Reading Check. What does it ask you to do?

4. Find another Quest. What is it called?

Learn to use important skills.

> **Read the explanation. Look at all the text and pictures.**

> **Practice the skill. You'll be ready to use it whenever you need it.**

Map and Graph Skills

Interpret Timelines

A timeline shows the order in which events happen. It can show how the present is connected to the past. You read a timeline from left to right, just like a sentence. The event that happened first, or earliest, is placed on the left part of the timeline.

Look at the timeline of this family. It shows some important events that happened to them over time. Some things about the family changed, while others stayed the same.

Each event is marked with a date. The date tells when the event happened.

Your Turn!

1. What does the timeline in this lesson show?

   INTERACTIVITY
   Review and practice what you learned about timelines.

   _____
   _____
   _____
   _____
   _____

2. **Circle** the event that happened in 2011.

3. Use a separate sheet of paper. **Create** a timeline of your life so far. Or, construct a timeline of your school day. Include important events that happened to you. **Write** the date or time that each one happened.

2008   2011   2013   2018

Your Turn!

Work with a partner.

1. Find another skill lesson. What skill will you learn? Talk about another time you might need that skill.

Every chapter has primary source pages.
You can read or look at these sources to
learn right from people who were there.

Find out what this source is about and who made it.

These questions help you think about the source.

🔍 **Primary Source**

Photograph: Dairy Farm

You've learned about the different resources that are needed to produce goods and services. There are natural, capital, and human resources.

Dairy farmers are producers. They raise cows to produce milk. Suppose you want to know what resources a farmer needs to raise cows.

The photograph below is a primary source that can help you know what is needed. Look carefully at the photograph. What does it show? Take turns asking each other questions about the picture.

Primary Source

Using a Primary Source

Look at the photograph to answer these questions.

1. What are some natural resources a farmer needs to raise cows?

2. What are some capital resources a farmer needs to raise cows?

3. Based on this photograph, what can you write about the size of a dairy farm?

Wrap It Up

Summarize what you learned about the resources a dairy farmer needs to raise cows.

This is the source.

Pull it all together.

2. Find another primary source lesson in your book. What is the source about?

Map and Graph Skills Handbook

Using Globes

Vocabulary

geography
globe
equator
latitude
longitude
legend
symbol
scale
compass rose
bar graph
flow chart

Geography is the study of land, water, and people on Earth. A **globe** is a round model of Earth. Look at these lines on the globe.

Equator: an imaginary line dividing Earth in half between the North Pole and the South Pole.

Latitude: imaginary lines that run east and west.

Longitude: imaginary lines that run north to south.

Latitude and longitude lines are used to find absolute location.

1. ☑ **Reading Check** Find the equator and latitude and longitude lines. **Run** your finger along one line and ask your partner to name the line.

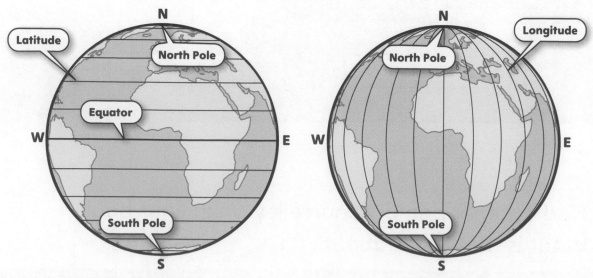

Using Maps

You can use a map to look closely at places, landforms, or bodies of water. Look for the following features on the map of Illinois.

Title: tells what the map shows and may show a date.

Map key, or legend: identifies symbols on the map.

Symbol: a marking that stands for something else.

Illinois, 2017

Legend
⊙ state capital
• other city

Scale: shows distance so you can see how far apart locations are.

Compass rose: shows directions using letters to stand for north, south, east, and west.

2. ☑ Reading Check **Underline** the date in the map's title. **Circle** the capital of Illinois. **Write** what direction you would mainly travel from Rockford to Bloomington.

_____

_____

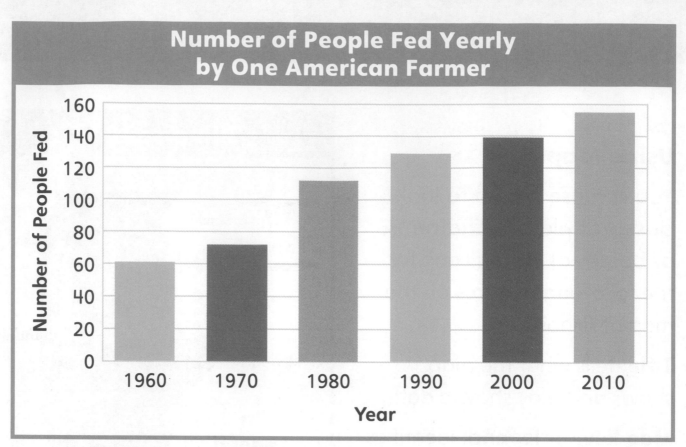

Number of People Fed Yearly by One American Farmer

Number of People Fed (vertical axis): 0, 20, 40, 60, 80, 100, 120, 140, 160

Year (horizontal axis): 1960, 1970, 1980, 1990, 2000, 2010

Source: American Farm Bureau Federation

Using Information

A **bar graph** uses bars to show information over time. Look at the title to find what it shows. Look at the side and bottom labels to find what information is included. Find 1980. Move your finger up the bar. It tells you that during 1980 about 110 people were fed by one farmer's crops.

3. ☑ Reading Check On the bar graph, **circle** the number of people fed by one farmer in 1960. **Underline** the year in which about 155 people were fed by one farmer.

The bar graph showed that the number of people fed by one farmer's crops has increased over the years. None of these crops could have grown without water or the water cycle. The water cycle is the process that reuses water. The water we have on Earth today is the same water that has been on Earth since it began.

You can follow the water cycle using a flow chart. A **flow chart** is a drawing that shows the sequence of how something works or how to do something. Notice the arrows in this flow chart. They keep going because the water cycle never stops.

4. ☑ **Reading Check**
   On the flow chart, circle what happens after water falls as rain. Underline what happens after water collects as clouds. Talk with a partner about what the arrows tell about the water cycle.

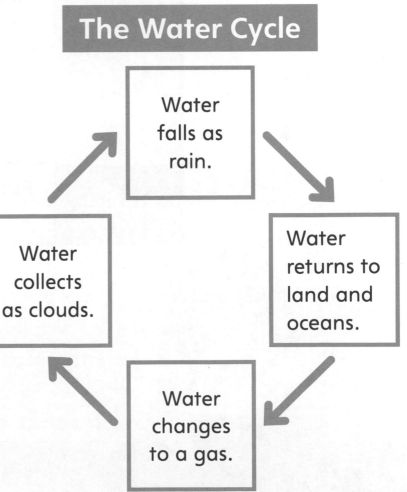

The Water Cycle

Water falls as rain.

Water returns to land and oceans.

Water changes to a gas.

Water collects as clouds.

Writing Workshop

Keys to Good Writing

Good writers choose a topic. They research their topic and take notes. Then they follow steps when they write. Here are five steps that will help you become a good writer!

Prewrite	Plan your writing.
Draft	Write your first draft.
Revise	Read and make your writing better.
Edit	Check your writing for spelling and grammar. Write a final draft.
Publish	Publish your writing to share with others.

Writing Genres

Opinion

An opinion is how you think or feel about a topic. Give reasons that explain your opinion. Also include facts from research that support your reasons.

Informative/Explanatory

Explain or describe a topic you know about or have researched. Start by writing the most important ideas. Also give supporting facts and details. You can add pictures and diagrams, too.

Narrative

Write a story to tell about an event or events. Put events in the order they happened. Also give details to describe actions, feelings, and thoughts.

1. ☑ Reading Check **Turn and talk** to a partner. **What could be a topic for each kind of writing?**

Using the Library Media Center

How do you research information to use in your writing? Start in the library media center. There are materials and books on many topics. Learn how they are organized so you can quickly find things. The librarian will also help you find what you need.

Look for more than one resource on the topic you are writing about. You may find books and magazines that have information. Be sure to note which resources you use. Using the library media center is an important tool in finding information to help you write.

2.  **Reading Check** **How can the library media center help you find information to use in your writing?**

_____

_____

_____

_____

3. ☑ **Reading Check** **What are topics that you would like to research?**

_____

_____

_____

_____

Using the Internet

The Internet is another way to find information.

- Choose key words that will help you find information on your topic.

- Ask the librarian or your teacher to help you find Web sites that have the proper information.

- Write the names of the sites you use. Make complete notes on the information.

Be Safe on the Internet

Some Web sites may be harmful.

- Watch out for computer viruses.

- Ask an adult to check the Web sites you find.

- Do not reply if a stranger contacts you. Tell an adult.

- Never give anyone on the Internet
  - your full name
  - your address
  - your phone number
  - your birthday

Using Primary and Secondary Sources

Vocabulary

primary source
journal
artifact
architecture
secondary
 source
biography
autobiography
historian

Primary Sources

Sources help us learn about people, places, and events from the past. A **primary source** is made or written by someone who saw or experienced an event. An eyewitness account is a primary source.

There are many other kinds of primary sources. A diary, or **journal**, is a daily record of thoughts and events in a person's life. Historical documents, or papers, can also tell about life in the past. These include letters and government records. An **artifact** is an object made and used by people. Maps, photographs, and artwork show us what people and places looked like in the past.

Architecture is also a primary source. Architecture means how buildings are designed. It can tell us about the people who use the buildings.

The U.S. Constitution is an important historical document. It is a primary source.

1. ☑ **Reading Check** Main Ideas and Details **Underline** three sources you can use to learn about the past.

Secondary Sources

Secondary sources teach us about the past, too. A **secondary source** is written or made by someone who did not see an event happen. Your textbook is a secondary source. Encyclopedias are also secondary sources. They collect information about a person, place, or event from other sources.

A book about a person's life written by someone else is called a **biography**. Biographies are secondary sources. An **autobiography** is a primary source. It is written by the person it is about.

A **historian** is someone who studies and writes about history. Historians use primary and secondary sources to learn about the past. Books and articles that historians write are secondary sources.

2. **☑ Reading Check** **Underline** the secondary sources. **Tell** a partner one question a biography about Abraham Lincoln could answer.

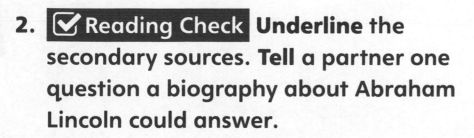

Many encyclopedias are on the Internet now.

Compare Primary and Secondary Sources

We can learn who, what, where, when, and how from primary and secondary sources. We can ask questions about sources to help us learn.

3. ☑ **Reading Check** **Look** at this photograph from the past. **Write** one question you have about the photograph.

To tell if a source is primary or secondary, ask this question: "Was the person there when the event happened?" If the person was there, the source is primary. Suppose you give a report on cars from a century, or 100 years, ago. Your report is a secondary source because you did not see or drive those cars. You did not live during that time.

An interview is another type of primary source. When a news reporter interviews the president, that interview is a primary source. Oral history, a recorded interview with someone from the past, helps us learn about history.

4. ☑ Reading Check Look at each source. **Write** a "P" below each primary source. **Write** an "S" below each secondary source.

biography of Harriet Tubman

castle architecture

photo of Jackie Robinson

encyclopedia

Families Today and in the Past

GO ONLINE FOR DIGITAL RESOURCES

▶ VIDEO

👆 INTERACTIVITY

🔊 AUDIO

🎮 GAMES

☑ ASSESSMENT

📖 eTEXT

The **BIG** Question

How does life change throughout history?

▶ VIDEO

Jumpstart Activity

👆 INTERACTIVITY

Families celebrate special occasions in different ways. Write something your family celebrates every year. In a small group, take turns acting out the celebration.

1 Start With a Brainstorm

INTERACTIVITY

Explore how life in the past was different from life today.

You can learn about the past by interviewing an older family member or neighbor. Think about questions you want to ask this person, such as *Did you do the same things that I do when you were in second grade? How has life changed since then?* Write down your ideas.

2 Look for Quest Connections

Turn to the lesson to begin looking for your Quest Connections.

3 Write Up Your Quest Findings

At the end of the chapter, use what you learned to make a poster and presentation about the person you interviewed.

I will know why it is important to learn about families.

INTERACTIVITY

Participate in a class discussion to preview the content of this lesson.

Vocabulary

family
community
responsible

Academic Vocabulary

respect

JumpStart Activity

Make a list of all the people who make up your family. Share your list with a partner.

What Does Family Mean to You?

A **family** is a group of people who live together and experience the world together. You may think of family as the people who care for you. They keep you safe and healthy. Your family may cheer you up when you are sad. You can count on your family. They are there for you when you need help. They teach you how to do new things.

1. ☑ **Reading Check** Write what family means to you.

_____

What Is a Community?

A **community** is a place where people live, work, and play together. We can also define community as a group of people who share the same interests and beliefs. The members of a community help each other. They care about each other's safety. Members of a community follow certain rules. Often, they work toward a common goal and have fun together.

A family is similar to a community. Members of a family care for one another. They follow the same rules. They have similar interests and beliefs, too. A family helps each other do chores. When they are done, a family has fun!

2. ☑ **Reading Check** Main Idea and Details **Highlight** ways people in a community help each other.

Why Is Learning About Family Important?

Learning about families is important because families are important! Your family may be the most important group to which you belong.

Your family helped you take your first steps. They taught you how to walk and talk. Who teaches you right from wrong? Your family! They teach you to treat others with **respect**.

People in your family help meet everyone's needs. Older members work to make money so that you have food to eat and clothing to wear. They make money so you have a home.

Academic Vocabulary

respect • being kind and fair to others

Your family makes a difference in your life. Family members teach you to be responsible. Being **responsible** means that you take care of important things. Your family teaches you to care for yourself and be independent.

3. ☑Reading Check **Look** at the pictures. **Circle** skills that families teach children.

INTERACTIVITY

Check your understanding of the key ideas of this lesson.

☑ **Lesson 1 Check**

4. **Main Idea and Details** Finish this sentence.
The people in my family make a difference

in my life because _____

_____

_____

5. **Draw** a picture on a separate sheet of paper. Show what a family member has taught you that helps you in your life.

6. **Draw Conclusions** How is a community of people similar to a family?

_____

_____

_____

Unlock The BIG Question

I will appreciate and respect all kinds of families.

INTERACTIVITY

Participate in a class discussion to preview the content of this lesson.

Vocabulary

extended family
generation
guardian
immigrant
citizen
tradition

Academic Vocabulary

practice

JumpStart Activity

Talk to classmates. Find someone with the same number of siblings or adults at home as you have.

What Makes a Family?

Every family is one of a kind! That is because the people who make up a family are special. Families can be large, with many adults and children, or they can be small, with only one parent and one child. Many families make up a community. It is nice to meet families who are different than yours. Treat each family you get to know with respect and kindness. Then they will do the same to you and your family!

How Are Families Organized?

Families are organized in different ways. An **extended family** includes more than parents and children, such as aunts and uncles. Some families have two or more generations living with them, including grandparents. A **generation** means people born and living about the same time.

Some families have one parent, a mom and a dad, two moms, or two dads. Some children have parents who live in different homes. Some children live in a family with a **guardian** who cares for them. Others are adopted by a family.

1. ☑ Reading Check **Tell** how many generations of people live with you.

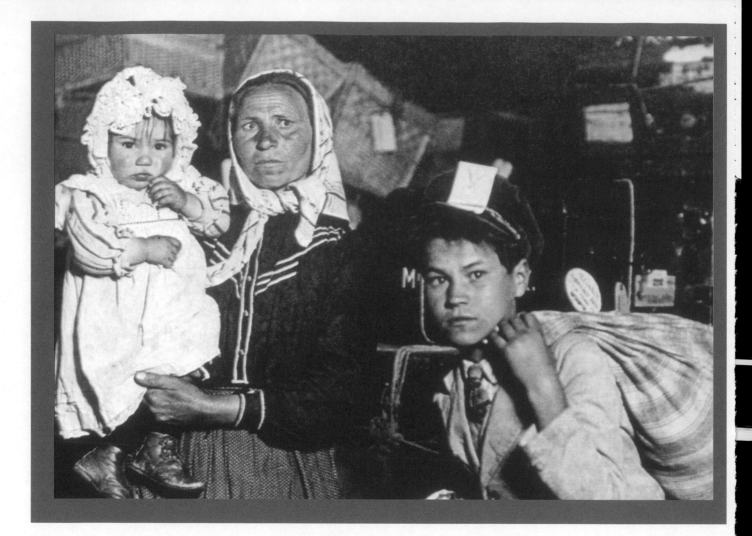

Immigrant Families

A person who moves from one country to another is called an **immigrant**. Many immigrant families leave their homes to make a better life in the United States. Some families want freedom to **practice** their religion. Others want to live in a country that is safe. Better jobs and schools may also bring people to the United States. In some cases, immigrants join family already living here.

Academic Vocabulary

practice • to follow teachings and rules

When they arrive, many immigrants want to become United States citizens. A **citizen** is a person who belongs to a country. Citizens have the right to live, work, and vote here. Immigrants can take a citizenship test. Then they take part in a ceremony to become new citizens.

Word Wise

Suffixes
You know what *citizen* means. What do you think *citizenship* means?

2. ☑ Reading Check **Circle reasons families from other countries move to the United States.**

Quest Connection

Who are older family members that you can interview to find out about important traditions? Write a list of their names.

👆 INTERACTIVITY

Explore examples of family traditions.

How Families Are Similar

Families from around the world bring traditions to the United States. A **tradition** is something that is passed down over time. Many traditions are similar. It is a tradition to eat special foods on holidays. Singing, dancing, and wearing formal clothing are traditions, too. Another tradition is practicing your own religion. Activities that are passed on from generation to generation are traditions, too. Older family members teach children what they believe in and value most in life. These traditions continue when families move to the United States.

Traditional Jewish wedding

3. ☑ **Reading Check** Compare and Contrast
Write ways families are alike and different.

_____

- -

_____

_____

- -

_____

_____

- -

_____

_____

INTERACTIVITY

Check your understanding of the key ideas of this lesson.

☑ **Lesson 2 Check**

4. On another sheet of paper, **draw** a picture
of what you consider to be your extended family.
Label the people in the picture.

5. Understand the _Quest_ **Connections Look** at the list of
people you made. **Circle** the name of the person
you want to interview.

Interpret Timelines

A timeline shows the order in which events happen. It can show how the present is connected to the past. You read a timeline from left to right, just like a sentence. The event that happened first, or earliest, is placed on the left part of the timeline.

Look at the timeline of this family. It shows some important events that happened to them over time. Some things about the family changed, while others stayed the same.

Each event is marked with a date. The date tells when the event happened.

2008

2011

1. What does the timeline in this lesson show?

INTERACTIVITY

Review and practice what you learned about timelines.

_____

_____

_____

_____

_____

_____

_____

2. Circle the event that happened in 2011.

3. Use a separate sheet of paper. **Create** a timeline of your life so far. Or, construct a timeline of your school day. Include important events that happened to you. **Write** the date or time that each one happened.

2013   2018

3 Life Then and Now

I will know that families have a history.

INTERACTIVITY

Participate in a class discussion to preview the content of this lesson.

Vocabulary

history
ancestor
culture

Academic Vocabulary

compare
contrast

JumpStart Activity

Work with a partner. Take turns acting out things you learned to do since you were little.

You Have a Past

History is the story of the past. It tells about people and events from long ago. It tells about places and objects, too. We use the words *yesterday* and *then* to talk about the past. When we talk about the present, we use the words *today* and *now*. The word *tomorrow* tells about the future.

1. ☑ **Reading Check** **Highlight** words that tell about the past. **Circle** words that tell about the present. **Underline** words that tell about the future.

You have a past, too. Do you know when you took your first steps? What were the first words you said? Learning how to walk and talk is part of your personal history. Using a fork and knife to eat and tying your shoelaces on your own are, too. Learning how to read, write, and add are important things to do. What are you learning how to do today? What do you want to learn how to do in the future? All of these activities are and will be a part of your own personal history!

2. **☑ Reading Check Look** at the pictures. **Circle** something you learned to do in the past. **Draw** a square around something you are learning to do today. **Draw** a star on something you could learn to do in the future.

Your Family Has a Past

Just like you, your family has a past. You can trace the history of your family by studying it. Ask questions about events that happened to your family. Some questions to ask are: *What was life like a decade—that is, ten years—ago? What activities did you do in second grade?* Your dad or your grandmother can tell you how life has changed over time. That is because they are from a different generation. They can also tell you how life has stayed the same.

Families needed food and clothing in the past. Today, families need the same things. However, they meet their needs in different ways. Some families grew food in gardens or sewed their own clothing. Today, most people shop in stores to buy food and clothing. You can **compare** and **contrast** your life to what their lives were like long ago.

Academic Vocabulary

compare • to see how two or more things are similar
contrast • to see how two or more things are different

3. ☑ Reading Check **Summarize** how life was different in the past.

_____

_____

_____

_____

_____

Families Then and Now

Quest Connection

What questions can you ask family members to learn about your family's history?

👆 **INTERACTIVITY**

Learn how to interview someone.

An **ancestor** is a relative who lived long before your grandparents. You may have ancestors who lived a century—that is 100 years—ago. Their way of life, or **culture**, was similar. It was different, too!

Clothing, hairstyles, manners, and the way people behaved were all more formal. Today, families are more casual in how they dress and act. Families in the past ate home-cooked meals each night. Today, families sometimes eat prepared, or precooked meals. Long ago, children played board games and listened to family members tell stories. Today, you may play games and listen to stories on a computer.

Like in the past, families practice religion. They have morals, which are beliefs about what is right and wrong. Families go to community festivals. They listen to music, watch parades, and celebrate together.

4. ☑ **Reading Check Look** at the picture of the boys from long ago. **Talk** to a partner about how the children are similar to and different from children today.

👆 **INTERACTIVITY**

Check your understanding of the key ideas of this lesson.

☑ **Lesson 3 Check**

5. **Compare and Contrast Write** how the present and past are similar and different. **Tell** how some things change over time, and some things stay the same.

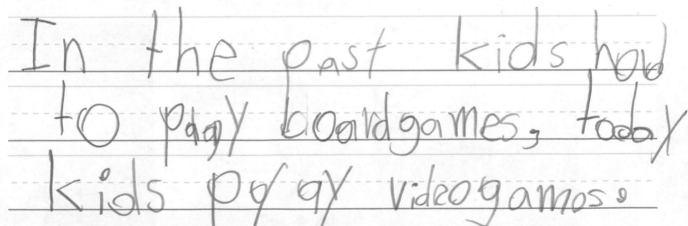

In the past kids had to play boardgames, today kids play videogames.

6. **Tell** what you learned to do when you were little. **Tell** what you are learning to do today. **Tell** what you want to learn to do in the future. Use the words *past*, *present*, and *future*.

7. **Understand the** *Quest* Connections **Write** a list of questions you can ask family members to learn more about your family's history. Use a separate sheet of paper.

Sequence

Sequence is the order in which things happen. We use clue words to tell about the order. Some clue words are *first*, *next*, and *finally*.

Look at the pictures and read the sentences. See how the sentences match the pictures.

Hugo is learning about family history in school. **First,** he talked with older members of his family.

Next, he looked at family photos from the past.

Finally, he wrote a report. Hugo told what he learned about his family's history.

Your Turn!

INTERACTIVITY

Review and practice what you learned about sequence.

1. **Read** the sentences and look at the pictures. **Write** *first*, *next*, and *finally* under the pictures to show the correct order. Then use your own words. **Tell** about the pictures in the sequence that they happened.

   First, Lea wrote questions to ask her grandfather.

   Next, she interviewed him.

   Finally, Lea gave a presentation to her class telling what she learned about the past.

finnay First ~~finnay~~ Next

2. **Draw** three pictures on a separate sheet of paper. Show three things you did today. Put the pictures in the correct sequence. **Write** *first*, *next*, and *finally* underneath the pictures. Then **tell** about each one.

Unlock The BIG Question

I will know how to use primary and secondary sources to learn about family history.

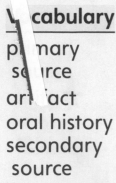

INTERACTIVITY

Participate in a class discussion to preview the content of this lesson.

Vocabulary

primary source
artifact
oral history
secondary source
family tree

Academic Vocabulary

examine

Jumpstart Activity

With a partner, find a classroom object that shows what life is like for a second grader. Tell the class what your object shows.

Different Kinds of Sources

You can learn about the past in many different ways. A **primary source** is one way. This is something written or made by a person who saw an event happen. Photographs and paintings are primary sources. An **artifact** is an object made long ago. You can learn about your family's past by talking to older family members. An **oral history** is recorded information from a person who experienced an event.

A **secondary source** is another way to learn about the past. This is written or made by someone who did not see or experience an event. Your social studies book is a secondary source. So is a biography of a person's life.

You can learn about people, places, and events from the past. Study different kinds of sources. They can show you how some things change over time. They also show how some things stay the same.

1. **☑ Reading Check** **Circle** the names of primary sources. **Underline** the names of secondary sources.

Let's see what we can learn from these artifacts, Kevin!

Grandpa Jones, what was life like for your dad?

Quest Connection

What kinds of artifacts can you study to trace your family history?

INTERACTIVITY

Explore how artifacts tell stories about the past.

Academic Vocabulary

examine • to study something closely and carefully

Learn About Your Family's History

How can you trace your family history? You can **examine** primary sources! Ask a family member to show you an artifact. It could be a war medal or jewelry worn by an ancestor. It could be a document, or written item, like a birth certificate or a train ticket. Postcards, letters, and diaries give clues about life in the past, too.

Interview or talk to an older family member. Record your conversation. Then you can listen to it in the future. You can also make a **family tree.** This drawing or diagram shows how family members are related.

2. **Reading Check** **Look at the family tree. Circle Kevin's parents.**

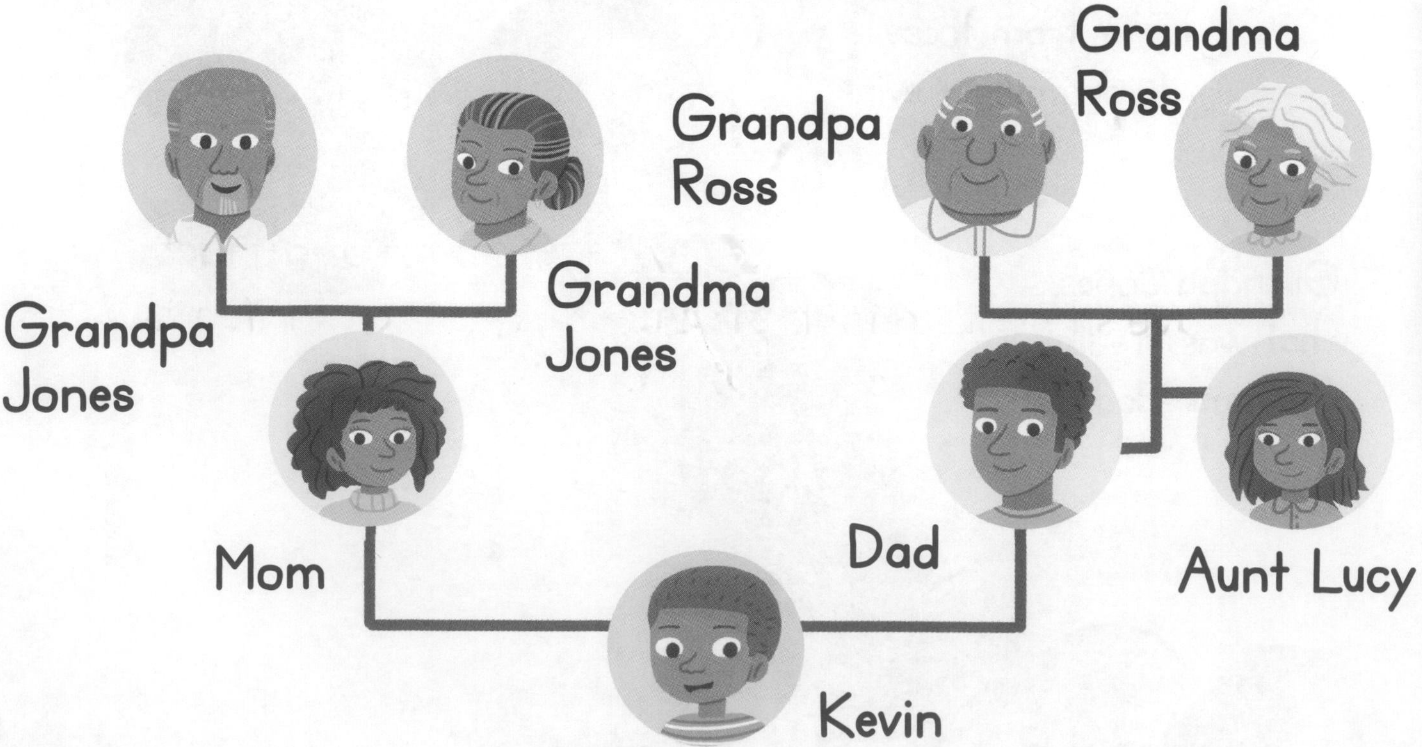

Grandpa Jones
Grandma Jones
Grandpa Ross
Grandma Ross
Mom
Dad
Aunt Lucy
Kevin

☑ Lesson 4 Check

3. Summarize how families can remember their past.

They can study primary sourcs like an artifact or photo they can interveiv a family nember

4. Write one way you can learn how life changes over time by studying primary sources.

I can look at photos to see how things chaged over time.

5. Understand the *Quest* **Connections** **Write** a list of artifacts you have seen at home that you want to ask your family member about. Use a separate sheet of paper.

Photograph: Angel Island

One kind of primary source is a photograph. You can study a photograph to find out the history of a family. It gives clues about people, places, events, and objects from long ago.

Look at the photograph that shows items from long ago. It was taken on Angel Island. This is in San Francisco Bay, California. Immigrants who wanted to move to the United States from Asia traveled by ship. Before they could enter the country, most of them had to stop here. They were asked questions and given a medical exam on Angel Island.

Primary Source

Using a Primary Source

1. **Look** at the photograph. **Circle** an artifact someone wore. **Draw a box** around a family photograph. **Draw an X** on a document.

2. **Talk with a partner.** Take turns asking and answering questions about the photograph. The questions can begin with *Who? What? Where? When? Why?* and *How?*

Wrap It Up

Summarize what you learned about the people who stayed at Angel Island.

The clothes show ther probly from South Korea. They have little bit of thing in the small suit case.

Quality:
Leadership

James Oglethorpe
Founder of Savannah, Georgia

James Oglethorpe was a strong leader in England. There he worked to change how prisoners were treated. He also looked for ways to help people with little money.

In 1732, King George II of England allowed Oglethorpe to start a new settlement in North America. It was named Georgia after the king. Oglethorpe led over 100 people on a two-month journey across the Atlantic Ocean. Once in Georgia, Oglethorpe planned the new town of Savannah. Many people think of Oglethorpe as the first governor of Georgia.

Write why James Oglethorpe was a strong leader.

he helped poor pep

Talk About It

Turn to a partner. Take turns telling about times when you showed leadership.

☑ Assessment

🎮 **GAMES**
Play the vocabulary game.

Vocabulary and Key Ideas

1. **Sequence** Write steps you can take to learn about and report on your family **history**.

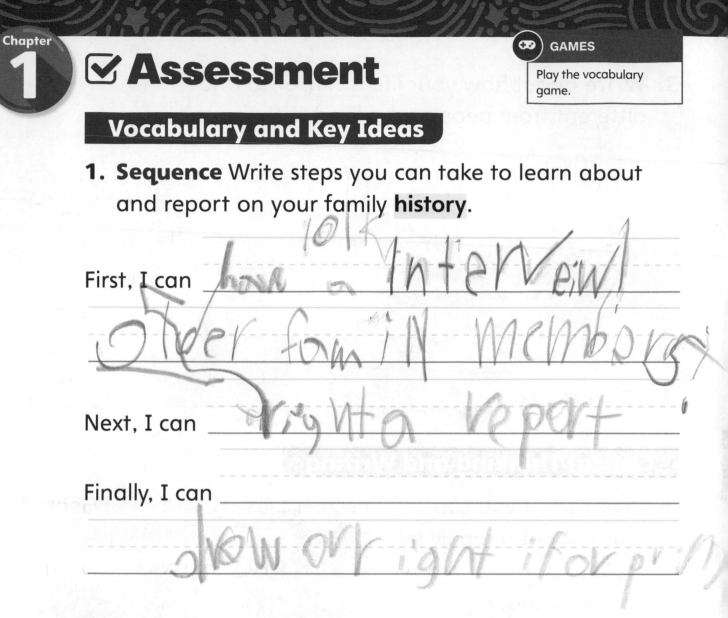

First, I can _____ hav a Interveiw older famliy membgrs

Next, I can _____ rigt a report

Finally, I can _____ show or right ifor p'

2. **Draw** a picture. Show a tradition you share with your family. **Tell** about who makes up your **family**.

3. **Write** about how your life is similar to and different from people who lived in the past.

Now we buy clothes in the
they made them all.

Critical Thinking and Writing

4. **Write** what you can learn about a family by looking at this primary source photograph.

Quest Findings

INTERACTIVITY

Use this activity to help you prepare your interview and poster.

Make a Poster

It is time to put it all together. Write questions, conduct an interview, and make a poster!

1 Prepare to Write

What questions will you ask a family member or neighbor? Remember, you want to learn about what life was like in the past and how it changed over time.

2 Write Interview Questions

Write your questions. They should begin with *Who? What? Where? When? Why?* and *How?*

3 Do Your Interview

Interview your person. Record it or take notes.

4 Make a Poster

Create a poster comparing life in the past with life today. Put the labels **Then** and **Now** at the top. Include a timeline on your poster.

5 Present Your Poster

Share your poster with the class!

Chapter 2

People, Places, and Nature

GO ONLINE FOR
DIGITAL RESOURCES

▶ VIDEO

👆 INTERACTIVITY

🔊 AUDIO

🎮 GAMES

☑ ASSESSMENT

📖 eTEXT

The BIG Question What is the world like?

▶ VIDEO

Lesson 1
Use Maps to Locate Places

Lesson 2
Earth's Land and Water

Lesson 3
Where People Live

Lesson 4
Our Communities and Resources

Jumpstart Activity

👆 INTERACTIVITY

Look at what the family is doing. Talk with a partner about some other outdoor activities you can do in your neighborhood. Then, if your teacher asks you to, get up and act out some of these activities.

AUDIO

Places Where We Live

by Charlotte Munez

Preview the chapter **vocabulary** by singing the song to the tune of "On Top of Old Smokey."

We live in big **cities**
And **suburbs** or **towns**.
These places are different
In their sights and their sounds.

Big cities and small towns
Are found everywhere.
A road or a highway
Will take you right there!

Quest
Project-Based Learning

Help a Geographer

Quest Kick Off

Hi! I'm Gina the geographer. I look at different types of land and how people use the land. Would you look at some places in our country with me? Think about what makes one environment a good place to live. Then give a talk about why it is a good place to live.

1 Start with a Brainstorm

Think about your community. What is it like? What do you do there? Describe it.

 **INTERACTIVITY**

Think about what your community has to offer that makes it a good place to live.

houses, trees, town
school, apartment, a
skyscraper building

2 Collect Clues for Quest Connections

Turn to the next page to begin collecting clues for your Quest connections.

3 Give Your Talk Quest Findings

At the end of the chapter, use what you learned to talk about the environment you chose and why it is a good place to live.

1 Use Maps to Locate Places

Unlock The BIG Question

I will know how to use maps to locate places.

INTERACTIVITY

Participate in a class discussion to preview the content of this lesson.

Vocabulary

relative location
absolute location
town
legend
city
compass rose

Academic Vocabulary

symbol

Jumpstart Activity

Think of a place in your school. Draw a map to help your partner find it.

Relative Location

Go outside. What do you see? Everything is in a certain place, or location. **Relative location** tells where something is by comparing it to something else. Words such as *near*, *behind* and *above* tell where people, places, and things are located.

1. ☑ **Reading Check** **Write** a sentence using a relative location word to tell about the fence in the picture.

My fence in front of the school!

My home address is 30 Main Street, Fremont, OH.

Absolute Location

The exact spot where a place is located is its **absolute location**. It may include a place's house number, street, town, and state. A **town** is a small community.

Imagine being invited to a friend's house. Your friend tells you the street address. So you know its absolute location. But how do you get there? You can use a map on the Internet. Type in your address and your friend's address with an adult's help. Directions will pop up telling you how to get there.

2. ☑ Reading Check Look at the picture. **Write the absolute location of this school.**

101, Main street, OH.

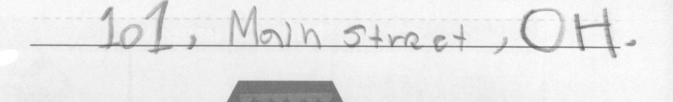

I'm standing next to the flag pole.

101

MAIN STREET

Map Grid of a Classroom

A map is a flat picture that shows where things are located. Maps help you find the relative and absolute location of things on the map. Some maps use lines called a grid. The lines divide the map into columns and rows to form boxes. Columns are labeled across the bottom with letters. Rows are labeled along the side with numbers. The box where a column and a row meet tells a place's location. So to find C-1, look at Column C, Row 1.

3. ☑ **Reading Check** **Circle** what is found in C-1 on the map grid. **Put an X on what is in B-2.**

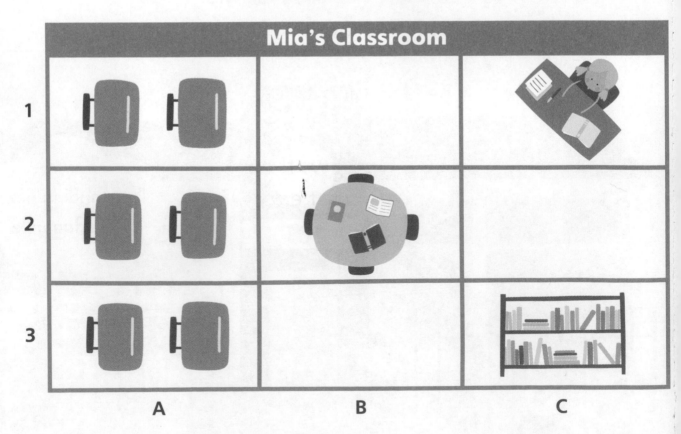

Mia's Classroom

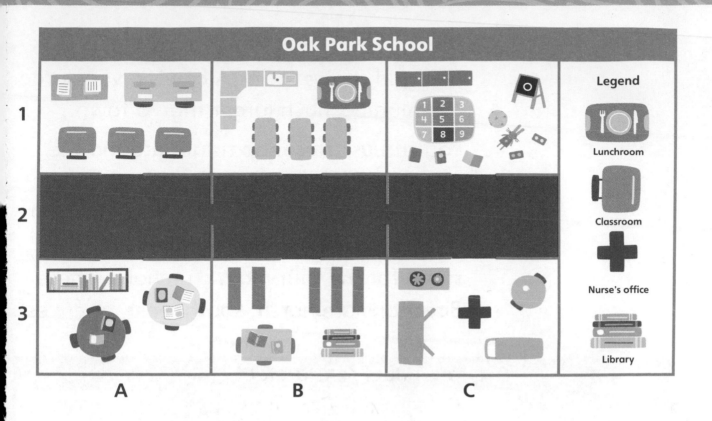

Map Grid of a School

Look at this map grid. The title tells what the map is about. This map shows some of the places inside Oak Park School. This map uses pictures to stand for real things. These small pictures are called **symbols**.

The map key, or **legend**, shows the different symbols. It tells what each means. One symbol is a lunch tray. It stands for the school's lunchroom.

4. ☑ **Reading Check** Look at the school map grid. **Circle** the title. **Draw** a line from each legend symbol to its location on the map.

Academic Vocabulary

symbol • an object that stands for something else

Map Grid of a City

This grid shows a city. A **city** is a very large community, much larger than a town.

You can use this map to get around the city. A **compass rose** shows directions on the map. It is a directional indicator. That is because a compass rose uses letters to stand for the four main directions. These directions are north, south, east, and west.

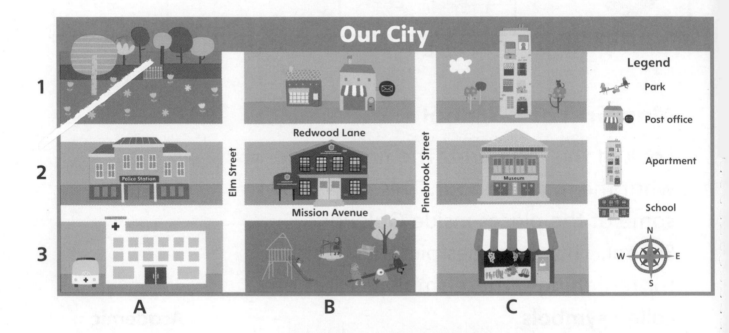

5. ☑ **Reading Check** **Main Idea and Details** Look at the map and use the compass rose and legend. **Write** S on a place that is south of the apartment. **Circle** the place that is west of the school. **Draw** a square around the place that is located in B-3.

☑ Lesson 1 Check

6. **Compare and Contrast Write** how absolute and relative location are different. Talk about it with a partner.

_____

_____

_____

_____

7. **Write** about the location of where you live using words that show relative location.

_____

_____

_____

8. Find the map grid titled "Our City."
   Point to the post office. Move east one square.
   What building is found there?

_____

_____

Using Map Scale to Ask and Answer Questions

A map is smaller than the place it shows. When you want to ask questions about distances on a map, you use a map scale. It lets you measure the distance between two places. You can ask *where* and *what* questions. Then use the map scale to answer the questions. Here is a present-day map of cities in New York.

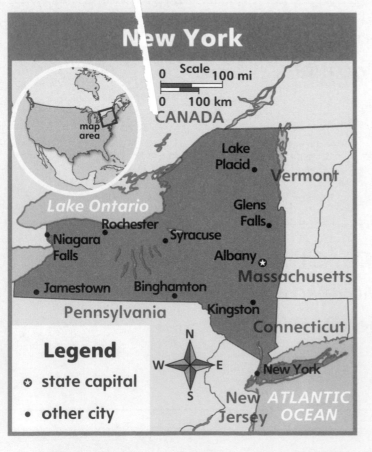

- The map scale stands for 100 miles. The green part at the top of the scale stands for 50 miles.

- Put a strip of paper next the dot for Lake Placid to next to the dot by Glens Falls. Mark each with a pencil.

- Put the strip of paper under the map scale with one dot at zero. The distance is about 100 miles.

1. **Write** the title for this map.

_____

_____

_____

INTERACTIVITY

Review and practice what you learned about map scale to ask and answer questions.

2. About what is the distance between Rochester and Syracuse? **Measure** and **write** it.

_____

_____

_____

3. **Ask** and **answer** your own question about the distance between two cities on the map. **Write** the question first. Then **measure** the distance. **Write** the distance.

_____

_____

_____

_____

_____

_____

_____

Earth's Land and Water

Unlock The BIG Question

I will know how to identify different kinds of land and water.

INTERACTIVITY

Participate in a class discussion to preview the content of this lesson.

Vocabulary

landform
ocean
continent
globe

Academic Vocabulary

model

JumpStart Activity

Create a symbol for a mountain and a river. Talk about them with a partner.

Landforms

Earth has different shapes of land. Each shape is called a **landform**. A mountain is the highest kind of land. The Sierra Nevada is a mountain range in California. A hill is a raised area. It is not as high as a mountain. A low area of land between mountains is a valley. Plains are flat areas of land.

1. ☑ **Reading Check** **Draw** a line from each landform picture to its name in the text.

mountains

valley

hills

plains

Bodies of Water

Earth's geography also includes many kinds of water. Each body of water has different features. An **ocean** is a large body of salt water. The Pacific Ocean is found along the western coast of the United States.

A river has fresh water. It is a long body of water that flows into another body of water. One river in Georgia is the Savannah River.

A lake has land on all sides. It has fresh water like a river. The Finger Lakes are examples of large lakes in New York.

2. ☑ Reading Check **Underline the name of the ocean along the western coast. Circle the name of a river in Georgia. Put an X on the name of the lakes in New York.**

lake

river

ocean

A Map of North America

You live on the continent of North America. A **continent** is a large land area on Earth. The United States, Mexico, and Canada are countries in North America. Canada is north of the United States, while Mexico is south of it.

Look at the map of some major landforms in North America. You can use a compass rose to find these landforms. The Appalachian Mountains are in the east. The Rocky Mountains are in the west.

Find the bodies of water on the map. The Atlantic Ocean lies on the east coast of North America. The Great Lakes are in the upper middle part of North America. They are near both the United States and Canada. The Rio Grande is a river in the southwest part of the United States.

Quest Connection

What kinds of land and bodies of water are there near where you live?

👆 **INTERACTIVITY**

Think about the land and water around you. Talk with a partner about how it makes your community a special place to live.

3. ☑ **Reading Check** Main Idea and Details Look at the map. **Underline** the map title. **Draw** a square around the name United States. **Circle** the Atlantic Ocean. **Draw** an **X** on the Mississippi River. **Draw** a **Y** on the Rocky Mountains.

North America

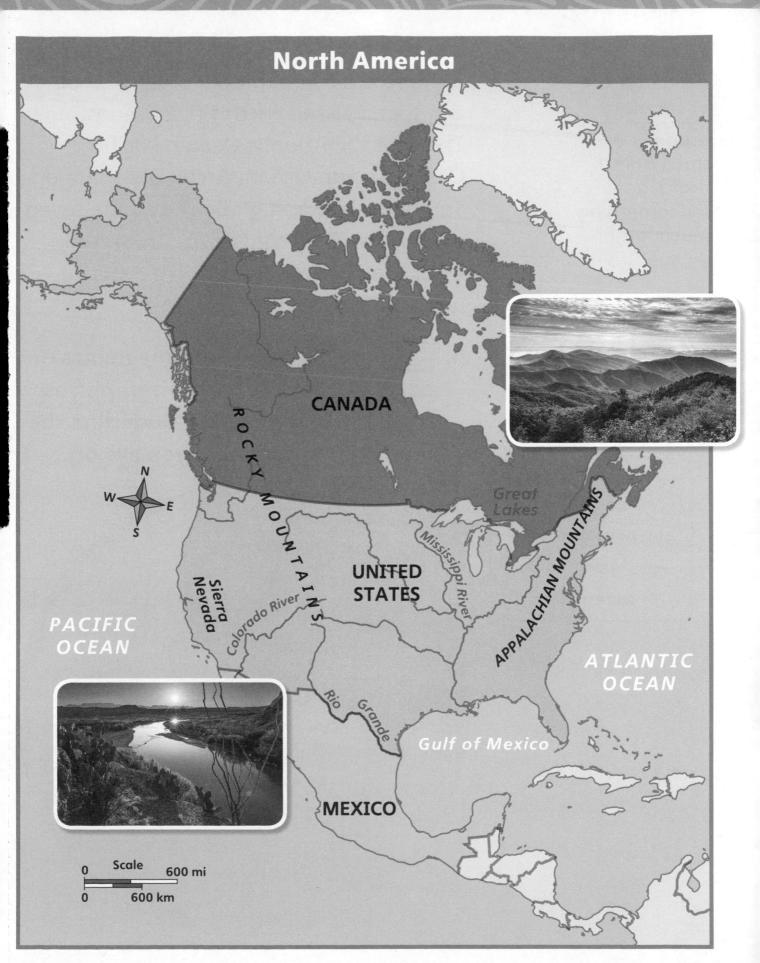

PACIFIC OCEAN

CANADA

ROCKY MOUNTAINS

Sierra Nevada

Colorado River

UNITED STATES

Mississippi River

Great Lakes

APPALACHIAN MOUNTAINS

ATLANTIC OCEAN

Rio Grande

Gulf of Mexico

MEXICO

N
W   E
S

Scale
0   600 mi
0   600 km

Earth's Shape

Academic Vocabulary

model • a small object that stands for something much larger

A **globe** is a round **model** of Earth. You can spin it to see Earth's five oceans. They are the Atlantic Ocean, Pacific Ocean, Indian Ocean, Arctic Ocean, and Southern Ocean. A globe shows the seven continents. They are Africa, Antarctica, Asia, Australia, Europe, North America, and South America.

4. ☑**Reading Check** Find the names of Earth's oceans in the paragraph you read. **Circle** the names. **Underline** the name of the continent you live on.

Legend

⊙ national capital

━━ national borders

─── state borders

CANADA

UNITED STATES

✪ Washington, D.C.

MEXICO

ATLANTIC OCEAN

PACIFIC OCEAN

☑ Lesson 2 Check

5. **Main Idea and Details Identify** landforms and bodies of water. Tell a partner about them.

6. Use the Outline Map of North America. **Find** countries, rivers, oceans, mountain ranges, and the Great Lakes. **Label** them from memory.

North America

7. **Understand the** *Quest* **Connections** On the list below, **underline** each type of land and water in your community: mountains, hills, valley, plains, ocean, rivers, lakes.

3 Where People Live

I will know how and why people have moved to the United States from other parts of the world.

👆 **INTERACTIVITY**

Participate in a class discussion to preview the content of this lesson.

Vocabulary

migrate
harbor

Academic Vocabulary

evidence

JumPstart Activity

Work in a group. Ask: Have you moved? How many times? Count up the numbers in a chart. Who moved the most?

Why People Move

People move, or **migrate**, from one place to another. Some move for a better life or to be safe. Others move for a new job. Some people have been forced to move.

Long ago, many people traveled on large ships to come to our country. They docked at harbors in places such as New York. A **harbor** is a safe place near land where ships are tied up. Soon after, they made their way to nearby cities and towns. Living near large cities helped people find jobs. It also helped them get things they needed.

Jackson, Mississippi

Over time, more and more people moved to all parts of the country to live, work, or have fun. Some of the land changed to meet their needs.

How People Move

People have moved from one place to another for thousands of years. Long ago, they used wagons. Today, people travel by car, train, ship, or airplane.

The family unpacking boxes moved from Ghana to the United States. The map shows the family's route.

1. ☑ Reading Check On the map **underline** the name of the country the family moved from. **Draw** a square around the name of the place the family moved to. Then in the text, **circle** the form of transportation the family used to get there. **Write** why you think they moved.

_____

_____

Ghana

Learning When, Why, and How People Move

Academic Vocabulary

evidence • facts and information that are true

You can gather **evidence** to find out when, why, and how people move. One way to do this is to talk to, or interview, family members about your ancestors.

During your interview, family members may show you on a globe where your ancestors lived and moved to. They may have objects you can learn from. For example, a ship ticket or photograph might show how and when people moved. A letter might give clues about why they moved.

Word Wise

Synonyms
You know what *gather* means. What is another word that means almost the same as *gather*?

2. ☑ **Reading Check** **Underline** how to locate where your ancestors lived and moved to. **Circle** an example of an object that shows why, how, or when they moved.

☑ Lesson 3 Check

3. Main Idea and Details Tell a partner why it might be helpful to live close to a city. Then talk about why people move from place to place.

4. Interview family members. **Write** a question to learn where your ancestors moved from and to. **Write** a question to learn when, how, and why they moved.

_____

_____

_____

_____

5. Look at a map or globe. **Point** to where your ancestors lived and moved. **Write** when, how, and why they moved. Talk about your interview with a partner.

_____

_____

_____

_____

Morris Schneider on Traveling to America

In an interview, Morris Schneider tells about moving from Poland to the United States in 1920. He was ten years old at the time. He and his family traveled by ship to Ellis Island in New York.

Vocabulary Support

awed, amazed

overwhelming, having very strong feelings

steerage, the lower deck where many passengers stayed

"When we got on the Rotterdam, we had a field day. One, I was never on ship before and . . . I was awed by it. It was overwhelming. All the people and boarding the ship, it was all a brand new experience. We left Rotterdam, we set sail and about a half hour after the ship started my sister got very sea sick. It took us fourteen days to cross the Atlantic and in the entire crossing, she was in steerage, and the only time she came up for a breath of fresh air was just about a half hour before we saw the Statue of Liberty."

Using a Primary Source

1. **Underline** why Morris Schneider was amazed.

2. **Circle** how Schneider and his family traveled.
   Highlight the ocean he traveled across.

3. Draw a picture to show how Schneider and his sister may have looked when they first saw the Statue of Liberty.

Wrap It Up

Summarize what you learned about the Schneider's travels.

Our Communities and Resources

I will know ways that people change the land in their community.

👆 **INTERACTIVITY**

Participate in a class discussion to preview the content of this lesson.

Vocabulary

environment
urban
suburb
rural

**Academic
Vocabulary**

resource

JumpStart Activity

Look at the city in the picture. Draw what you think a city should look like. Share your drawing with a partner.

Urban Environment

The air, land, water, and life around us is called the **environment**. It is everything that makes up where we live. This includes people, plants, animals, and buildings. People change the land where they live to meet their needs. They change it to make their lives better, too.

A city and the places around it make up an **urban** environment. Here people change the land for buildings and streets. They cut down trees and make the land flat. They build strong parts below the ground to support tall buildings called skyscrapers.

Many people move to the city and live in apartments. They enjoy restaurants, museums, plays, and parks. Many people work in the city. They may walk, or ride bikes, or take a bus or subway to work. They care for the environment by not driving cars and making the air dirty.

1. ☑ **Reading Check** Use Evidence From Text **Underline** in the text details about how people change the land to build an urban community.

Word Wise

Compound Words
What are two smaller words in *skyscraper*? What does each word mean?

Suburban Environment

A **suburb** is a community that is near a city. A suburb has fewer people than a city, so it is less crowded. There are also fewer tall buildings. Many people live in single-family houses. Children can walk to school. People can ride their bikes to the grocery store.

People who live in many suburbs are close enough to a city to drive to work or to a museum. They are close to open space. It might be just a short drive to hike at a state park. Or, they might be able to go swimming or fishing in the ocean!

People clear land to build suburbs. Look at the photo taken from above of a suburb.

Notice the rows of houses on the land. These houses are close together, but each one still has a front and back yard. Some of the land around the houses is kept natural, too, so there are lots of trees and green areas for children to play.

In the suburbs, there are many streets and roads. Some roads lead to highways, bridges, and tunnels. They make it easy for people to travel through the suburbs and to nearby cities.

2. ☑Reading Check Summarize **Write how people change and make good use of the land in a suburb.**

_____

_____

_____

_____

_____

Rural Environment

A **rural** environment is made up of small towns and farms with some family-run stores. Fewer people live here than in a suburb or city. There is a lot of open space.

In a rural environment, people change the land and use **resources** like water and soil. Writer Jack London, who lived in California, said of the soil:

Primary Source

"I believe the soil is our greatest asset [benefit]."

—Jack London, 1914

Many farmers clear the land. Then, they use the soil to plant seeds and grow crops for food. They supply water to the land so the crops can grow.

3. **☑ Reading Check** Use Evidence From Text **Underline** in the text how farmers use and benefit from the land.

Academic Vocabulary

resource • something that people use

Quest Connections

How are the types of environments alike and different?

INTERACTIVITY

Think about what the environments have in common and what makes each one special.

Moving to a New Environment

Pretend that you are moving from a town to a city. You will want to learn about it first. You can use the Internet. Type keywords like the name of the city. Look in the library, too. Find books, maps, or photos that tell about the city.

INTERACTIVITY

Check your understanding of the key ideas of this lesson.

☑ Lesson 4 Check

4. **Compare and Contrast Write** how land use is alike and different in urban, suburban, and rural environments.

_____

_____

_____

_____

_____

_____

5. Talk with a partner about ways people change the land.

6. **Understand the Quest Connections** Draw a picture of one type of environment. Use another sheet of paper.

Summarize

When you summarize, you use your own words to tell about the main idea. You also use your own words to describe important details.

Read the paragraph below. The main idea is underlined. The details are highlighted.

It's time to pick strawberries on a rural farm in Plant City, Florida, and then make some tasty food! You can make jam and store it in glass jars. A fruit pizza with a pie crust is also yummy. Or, you can make a smoothie by blending yogurt and strawberries.

Summary

The next paragraph summarizes what you have just read about picking strawberries. The information it gives is called a summary.

You can pick farm-fresh strawberries and make some tasty treats. You can use strawberries to make smoothies, fruit pizza, and jam.

Your Turn!

1. Read the paragraph below. **Circle** the main idea. **Underline** the details.

👆 **INTERACTIVITY**

Review and practice what you learned about summarizing.

Helping Georgia's Bees

People in Georgia have found that millions of bees are in trouble, and they are working to save them. Bees are being hurt and sometimes killed by the chemicals some farmers use to help their crops grow. Chefs, restaurant owners, and others in the state are working to teach how harmful using chemicals on crops can be. They want farmers to use fewer treatments on their crops.

2. Write a summary of the paragraph in your own words.

_____

_____

_____

_____

_____

_____

Quality:
Problem Solving

George Washington Carver
Creator of New Products

George Washington Carver grew up in Missouri. As a little boy, he learned how to draw and made pictures of plants. George grew up to be a teacher and a scientist.

George knew that farmers should not always plant cotton because it harmed the soil. He taught them to plant other crops that kept the soil richer. So the farmers were able to grow more crops. He found good uses for the land. He created new products from sweet potatoes and peanuts, such as oil, paint, and coffee.

Farmers had problems getting the best use of their land. How did George Washington Carver help them solve this problem?

_____

_____

_____

_____

Talk About It

Turn and talk to a partner. Take turns telling about ways you solved a problem you had.

☑ Assessment

Vocabulary and Key Ideas

1. **Draw** a box around the legend. **Circle** the scale. **Measure** the distance between Atlanta and Macon. **Write** the relative location of the Atlantic Ocean to Georgia.

_____

_____

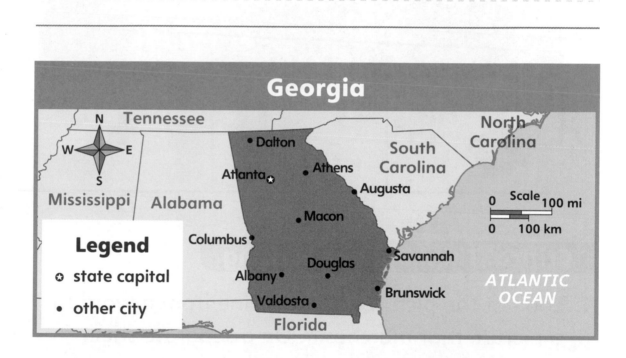

2. Jen's ancestors came from another country. **Circle** the object that Jen could use to learn when and how her ancestors came to the United States. **Underline** the object that would show her from where they came.

   a map of California

   a ship ticket dated 1855

   a map of Asia

3. Look at the map grid of the school. **Draw** a
square around the place that is located in C-1.
Use the Legend to find the library. **Circle** it.

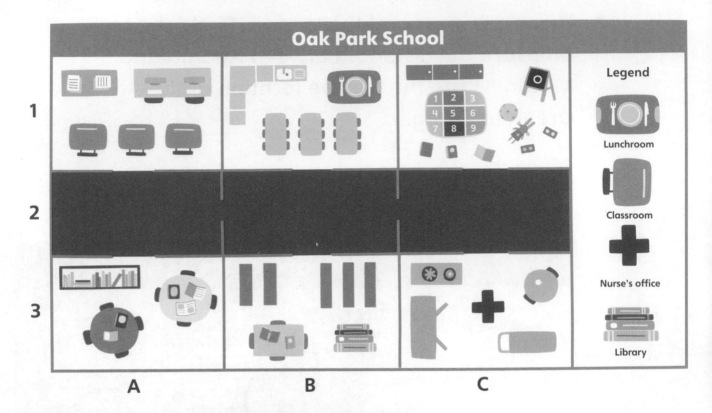

Critical Thinking and Writing

4. Look at the pictures. **Draw** a line from a word to
a picture that matches it. On a separate sheet
of paper, write about each type of environment
and its features.

urban   rural   suburban

Quest Findings

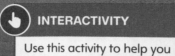

INTERACTIVITY

Use this activity to help you prepare to give your talk.

Give a Talk

It is time to put it all together to give your talk.

1 Get Ready to Talk!

Think about the different environments you learned about. What makes an environment a good place for you to live?

2 Get Set to Talk!

Plan how you want to describe the environment you chose. Make a poster. Use pictures and captions to show what makes it special and what you can do there.

3 Give Your Talk!

Use your poster to help you remember what you want to share about the environment you chose. Show it to your classmates as you tell your reasons and explain why it is a good place to live. Say your words in a way that shows you believe what you are saying.

GO ONLINE FOR
DIGITAL RESOURCES

- ▶ VIDEO
- 👆 INTERACTIVITY
- 🔊 AUDIO
- 🎮 GAMES
- ☑ ASSESSMENT
- 📖 eTEXT

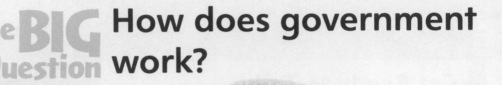

The **BIG** Question

How does government work?

▶ VIDEO

Lesson 1
Citizens Follow
Rules and Laws

Lesson 2
Our Government

Lesson 3
Governments
Around the World

Lesson 4
Governments Work
Together

JumPstart Activity

👆 INTERACTIVITY

Work with a partner. Take turns acting out and guessing rules you follow at home. Then do the same for rules you follow in school. Talk about why you need to follow these rules.

AUDIO

Our Country Today

Preview the chapter **vocabulary** by singing the song to the tune of "Rockabye, Baby."

When people vote
They each make a choice
We are all citizens.
We have a voice.

We elect people
To serve and to lead.
With honesty and fairness
In action and deed.

Chapter 3 Quest
Project-Based Learning

Help a School Leader

Quest Kick Off

Hi! I'm Principal Perry. I'm making a list of school rules. Would you help me decide if they are needed?

Think about rules you follow. Then you can show in a skit what school would be like without them.

NO PUSHING

1 Start with a Brainstorm

Make a list of rules you follow on the playground or in the classroom. Ask: *Is this rule important? What if we didn't have this rule? Would we remember what to do?*

👆 **INTERACTIVITY**

Think about why rules are needed and what might happen without them.

_____

_____

_____

_____

_____

_____

_____

2 Collect Clues for *Quest* Connections

Turn to the next page to begin collecting clues for your Quest connections.

3 Write Your Skit
Quest Findings

At the end of the chapter, use what you learned to write a skit and act it out. If possible, you may make a video of it too.

NO CLIMBING ON TREES

Citizens Follow Rules and Laws

I will know why rules and laws are important to follow at home and in school.

INTERACTIVITY

Participate in a class discussion to preview the content of this lesson.

Vocabulary

right
law
court

Academic Vocabulary

consequence

JumPstart Activity

Draw a picture showing how you share and work in a group. Talk about your picture with a partner.

Rules at Home

Think of the rules your family follows. Clean up your own mess. Ask before you go out. Help with tasks when asked. Tell the truth. Say "please" and "thank you." It is important for your family to have rules. They help everyone stay healthy and safe.

1. ☑ **Reading Check** Main Idea and Details **Underline** why rules are important at home.

Rules at School

Some school rules help you learn and work in a group. Others keep you safe. Your teacher makes the class rules. The class might help create a new rule or change one too.

Rules help keep things fair. How would your life be different if everyone in class talked at the same time? Your ideas might never be heard. That is why children raise their hand for a turn.

Think about playing kickball on the playground. What would happen if one person decided to always kick the ball? Other children would not get to play— the game would not be fun!

2. ☑ **Reading Check** **Cause and Effect Circle** **what happens when someone doesn't follow game rules.**

Rights, Responsibilities, and Laws

Every day you play and work in your home, school, and community. You have rights and responsibilities in these places. A **right** is something we are free to do. One right is to be treated fairly. Another is to be able to say what we think. We should all respect the rights of others.

We are responsible to follow laws. A **law** is a rule we obey. Our country makes laws to protect our rights and keep us safe. One law in our state is that everyone in a car must wear a seat belt. In some communities, only service or guide dogs are allowed on school grounds.

3. ☑Reading Check **Underline** rights that you have. **Circle** why the country makes laws.

Quest Connection

People follow rules, and they have responsibilities and rights. Think about how these are different.

👆 **INTERACTIVITY**

Talk with a partner about how rules, responsibilities, and rights might be connected. Why are they all important?

Consequences

Laws are made and carried out. One law says businesses must keep the air clean. A business that does not follow the law may have to pay a fine. That is one **consequence** for not carrying it out. Another consequence might be to go to court. A **court** is a place where people decide if someone has broken a law.

Academic Vocabulary

consequence • something that happens as a result of an action

INTERACTIVITY

Check your understanding of the key ideas of this lesson.

✓ Lesson 1 Check

4. **Cause and Effect Highlight** the consequences of not following a country law.

5. Why should we follow laws?

_____

_____

_____

_____

_____

6. **Understand the** *Quest* **Connections Draw** a picture. Show what would happen if people did not follow school rules or our country's laws.

Cause and Effect

A cause is what makes something happen. An effect is what happens. To find the cause, ask: *Why did this happen?* To find the effect, ask: *What happened?* Sometimes there is more than one cause or effect.

Look at the pictures. They show a cause and two effects.

Cause **Effect** **Effect**

You can fill in a chart to show cause and effect.

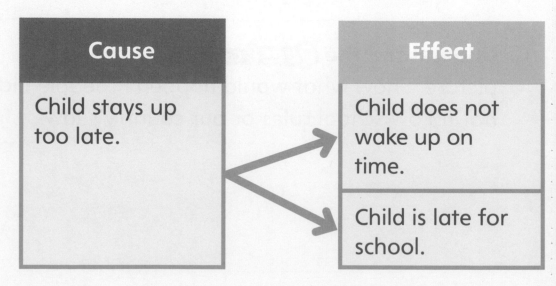

Cause		Effect
Child stays up too late.	→	Child does not wake up on time.
		Child is late for school.

Your Turn!

Read the paragraph below. **Circle** the cause. **Underline** the effects.

👆 **INTERACTIVITY**

Review and practice what you learned about cause and effect.

Earth Day

Years ago, people did not know that trash could hurt Earth. They littered and did not pick it up. On April 22, 1970, the first Earth Day took place. People wanted to tell others that it was important to keep Earth clean. Soon laws were passed to protect Earth. Now people celebrate Earth Day every year to remind us to take care of our environment.

Earth Day

Write the cause and effects in the chart.

Cause	Effect

Lesson 2 Our Government

Unlock The BIG Question

I will know how my government works.

INTERACTIVITY

Participate in a class discussion to preview the content of this lesson.

Vocabulary

government
constitution
Congress
vote
represent
tax
Supreme Court

Academic Vocabulary

interpret

JumpStart Activity

Play "Clue Me In" with a partner. Say a clue about something you think the government does. Have your partner guess what it is. Then switch roles.

What Is a Government?

A **government** is a group of people who work together to run a community, state, or country. A community government runs a city or town. A state government makes decisions for its communities. A country government works for its citizens. Some schools have a student government, which may help solve problems. Most governments have a **constitution**, which tells how the government works.

The United States Constitution created three parts, or branches of government. Each part has certain responsibilities. No branch has more power than another, so they work together to get things done.

President

The president is the leader of our country. The president lives and works at the White House in Washington, D.C. The president suggests and signs, or approves, new laws. People who work with the president help to carry out, or enforce, the laws. They do this by making sure that people obey laws.

The president is the leader of the military. Other leaders give advice to the president about important issues. These issues include education, health, and safety.

1. ☑ **Reading Check** **Summarize**
Underline responsibilities of the president.
Circle what the people who work with the president do.

Congress

Congress is the branch of government that makes and votes on laws. To **vote** means to make a choice that can be counted. Members of Congress work in the Capitol, a building in Washington, D.C. People in each state vote for their members of Congress. These members **represent**, or speak for, the people of their state. Look at the chart to learn more about the two parts of Congress.

| Members of Congress ||
Senate	House of Representatives
Two senators from every state	Number of people elected from each state is based on how many people live in the state
100 senators	No more than 435 representatives total
Elected every six years	Elected every two years

Congress is responsible for collecting taxes. A **tax** is money that is collected by the government from its citizens. Taxes help to pay for government services.

Both parts of Congress must vote on a bill before it can become a law. Then it is sent to the president. The president may say yes or no to the law. If the president says no, this means Congress has been checked. The president looked at the law and decided it was not good for the country. If the president signs the law, then the president thinks it will help the country.

2. **☑ Reading Check** **Underline** how Congress makes a law. **Circle** how the president checks Congress.

Word Wise

Multiple Meaning Words

A bill is paper money. A bill is also an idea that is written down for the government to decide on.

Quest Connection

What might happen if Congress did not make laws for our country?

INTERACTIVITY

Think about why laws are needed. Talk with a partner about the consequences if Congress is not able to do its job.

Supreme Court

The court system is another branch of government. State and local courts mainly decide if a law has been broken and, if so, the punishment. National level courts decide issues between states and laws for the whole country.

The **Supreme Court** is the country's highest court. It makes sure laws are fair by studying and **interpreting** the Constitution. Sometimes the Supreme Court may check Congress when it says a law is not fair. It may check the president when it says an action taken goes against the Constitution.

The Supreme Court has nine justices. The president picks each justice, but the Senate must agree to each choice. The Senate checks the president when it turns down one of those choices to the court.

Academic Vocabulary

interpret • make sense of or give meaning to

3. ☑ Reading Check **Underline how the Supreme Court checks Congress. Circle how the Senate checks the president.**

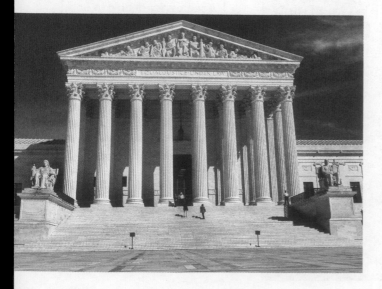

☑ Lesson 2 Check

4. **Compare and Contrast Write** how each branch of government works with laws.

Branches of Government	
President	
Congress	
Supreme Court	

5. Work with classmates. **Act out** jobs that each branch of government does.

6. **Understand the** *Quest* Connections **Write** why Congress makes laws and why it is important. Talk about it with a partner.

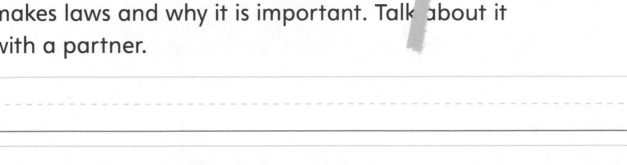

3 Governments Around the World

I will know why countries need government and what America's government is about.

INTERACTIVITY

Participate in a class discussion to preview the content of this lesson.

Vocabulary

independence
colony
freedom

Academic Vocabulary

document

JumpStart Activity

Work in a small group. Together, make a poster to show how a classroom government might be set up. Talk about your ideas with the class.

Why Countries Need Government

Most governments help their citizens by making laws to protect rights and property. The best governments work hard so their countries have success.

Governments make laws for safety, such as setting speed limits. Police officers carry out laws with the help of cameras and other tools to catch speeders. Most people who drive too fast get a ticket. Drivers who do something more serious go to court.

Citizens in the United States vote and elect leaders. These leaders follow the laws of our Constitution. In some countries, people do not choose their leaders. For example, kings or queens may rule a country because their parents were leaders.

Other countries are ruled by one person who takes over. In these places, the leader decides what the law is and if it has been broken. This leader also decides what the punishment is. People may have few rights. Other countries may be ruled by a group of powerful people. Few people are allowed to make changes in this form of government.

1. ☑**Reading Check** **Underline** reasons countries make laws. **Circle** how police officers carry out laws. Talk with a partner about what may happen in countries ruled by one person.

The Declaration of Independence

Long ago, people in our country were ruled by England. But the people did not want to be ruled this way. They wanted **independence**. They wanted to choose their own leaders to represent them. These people lived in 13 different colonies. A **colony** is a place that is ruled by a country far away.

Word Wise

Suffix:
You know what *colony* means. What is a *colonist*?

Thomas Jefferson, standing, wrote the Declaration of Independence. He worked with other leaders such as Benjamin Franklin, on the left, and John Adams, who offered ideas for changes.

The colonists wanted freedom. **Freedom** is the right to choose what we do and say. They asked Thomas Jefferson, an American leader, to write a **document** telling their reasons for separating from England and declaring their independence. He wrote the Declaration of Independence. In it, Jefferson said:

Academic Vocabulary

document • an official paper that proves something

Primary Source

"We hold these truths to be self-evident [easy to see], that all men are created equal. . . ."

—Thomas Jefferson, The Declaration of Independence, 1776

The document said that the colonists were free from England. Our country's leaders agreed to it on July 4, 1776.

2. **☑ Reading Check** Cause and Effect **Write** the cause.

Cause	Effect
	Thomas Jefferson wrote the Declaration of Independence.

The Constitution and Bill of Rights

England did not want the colonists to break away to form their own country. It did not want them to be free. So the colonists fought to gain their independence, and England fought to keep them as colonies.

The colonists did win their independence, though. They called their new country the United States of America. Then our country's leaders formed a government for the nation. But the government turned out to be too weak. So the leaders decided they needed a new plan. They wanted a plan that was strong but that did not take away freedoms. So they created the United States Constitution, which is our country's plan of government.

3. ☑ **Reading Check** **Underline the reason the United States Constitution was created.**

The Constitution includes the Bill of Rights. It lists 10 rights that protect our freedoms and that are shared by all citizens. These include being free to say and write what we want as long as it does not hurt anyone. Also, we are free to practice any religion we choose. We are free to join in a group to speak for or against issues, to vote, and to get a fair trial.

INTERACTIVITY

Check your understanding of the key ideas of this lesson.

☑ Lesson 3 Check

4. **Compare and Contrast Read** how some leaders come to power: just take over, are elected, or rule because their parents ruled. Fill in the

   blank. Leaders in the United States _____.

5. **Write** about a freedom you have and why it is important.

   _____

   _____

   _____

   _____

6. Why does the Constitution include the Bill of Rights?

   _____

   _____

Solve a Problem

Sometimes countries do not agree with each other. The same is true for people. When this happens, they need to find solutions, or ways to solve their problems. Often there will be more than one solution.

Zach's class is raising money for a food drive. What can he do to earn money to help buy food?

1. Identify the problem.
2. Find information to help solve it.
3. List some ways to solve it.
4. Identify the consequences of each way.
5. Try a solution.
6. Think about how the solution worked.

Look at the picture. Zach earned money by walking dogs. Work with a partner. Follow each step. Find your own solution to earn money to help a community group.

Your Turn!

INTERACTIVITY

Review and practice what you learned about solving problems

1. A nearby pond smells. It has trash around it. What is the problem?

_____

- -

_____

2. What information will help you solve the problem?

_____

- -

_____

3. Look at the picture. This is one solution. Talk with a partner about it and any other solutions. What are some consequences?

4. **Draw** a picture of your solution.

```



```

5. Talk with a partner about your solution.

Governments Work Together

**Unlock
The BIG
Question**

I will know
how our
government
works
with other
governments to
solve problems.

INTERACTIVITY

Participate in a class
discussion to preview the
content of this lesson.

Vocabulary

trade
peace

**Academic
Vocabulary**

conflict

JumPstart Activity

Work in a small group. Act out how you
work together to solve problems.

Countries Solving Problems

Countries want to get along so they find ways
to solve problems. Sometimes they trade to get
along because trade is important to countries.
To **trade** is to buy, sell, or exchange things.
Trading helps countries learn to work together.

Sometimes countries hope problems between
them will end if they learn about each other's
culture. They have concerts and art showings.
They offer exchange programs. This means
students from one country go to school in
another country for a certain length of time.

1. ☑ **Reading Check** **Underline** how trade
helps countries solve problems.

The United Nations

The United Nations was created more than 60 years ago to help countries work together to keep peace and stay safe. **Peace** means freedom from fighting or war. So the United Nations helps resolve, or end, problems. It also helps to better, or improve, human rights. Human rights are the freedoms that every person should have. The United Nations also helps poor countries make health conditions better so people stay well.

2. ☑**Reading Check** **Cause and Effect Highlight** why the United Nations was created.

Word Wise

Antonym: The word *united* means "joined together." What is a word that means the opposite of *united*?

Ways Leaders Solve Problems

World leaders practice diplomacy. This means they are careful about others' beliefs as they work toward keeping good relations among different governments. They listen to what others say. Then they use skill in dealing with problems to reach decisions that most everyone can agree on.

Some problems, or **conflicts**, are solved through a treaty. A treaty is an agreement between two or more nations. A treaty might end a war or set trade rules. It might tell where one country ends and another country begins.

Sometimes countries try to solve problems by using military force. The United States has done this to protect our beliefs and safety and to protect the human rights of people in other countries.

3. ☑ **Reading Check** Use Evidence From Text **Highlight** details about ways leaders use diplomacy to solve problems.

Academic Vocabulary

conflict • serious disagreement

☑ Lesson 4 Check

4. Complete this sentence: The United States and England wanted to end the war about America's freedom. So the two countries signed a

_____

_____

_____

5. Draw Conclusions Write about a time when a country might use military force. Talk about it with a partner.

_____

_____

_____

_____

_____

_____

_____

6. Two countries want to trade the same things. There are not enough people who want to buy them. Should they use diplomacy, stop trading, use military force, or make a treaty? **Underline** the two best ways.

Photograph: Panama Canal Treaty Signing

The United States built a waterway, or canal, in Panama during the early 1900s. It connected the Atlantic and Pacific Oceans. The United States knew Panama should be in charge of the canal, so the leaders of both countries signed a treaty giving Panama control.

Look at the photograph. It is a primary source. It shows President Jimmy Carter on the left, shaking hands with the ruler of Panama, Omar Torrijos Herrera, on the right, after they signed the treaty. What does it tell you about ways countries solve problems?

Primary Source

Using a Primary Source

1. **Write** *Who? What? Where? When? Why?*
   and *How?* questions about the photograph.
   Ask and answer them with a partner.

   _____

   _____

   _____

   _____

2. **Circle** the parts of the picture that show the leaders
   are happy with the treaty.

Wrap It Up

Summarize what you learned about how the United States
and Panama solved the problem of the Panama Canal. **Tell** a
partner what the United States had to give up for the treaty.
What was one good result from the treaty?

   _____

   _____

   _____

Quality:
Patriotism

Eleanor Roosevelt
Supporter of Human Rights

Eleanor Roosevelt was married to President Franklin Delano Roosevelt. Eleanor was patriotic, which means she loved her country. She helped children, women, the poor, and people of color. She worked so people could be healthy, safe, and treated fairly.

Eleanor helped write the Universal Declaration of Human Rights for the United Nations. She traveled around the world to help improve people's lives. She encouraged world peace, too.

Write about how Eleanor Roosevelt was patriotic.

_____

_____

_____

_____

_____

_____

Draw to Learn

Draw a picture to show how you are patriotic. Use a separate sheet of paper.

☑ Assessment

Vocabulary and Key Ideas

1. Look at the chart. It shows a cause and one effect. **Write** another effect.

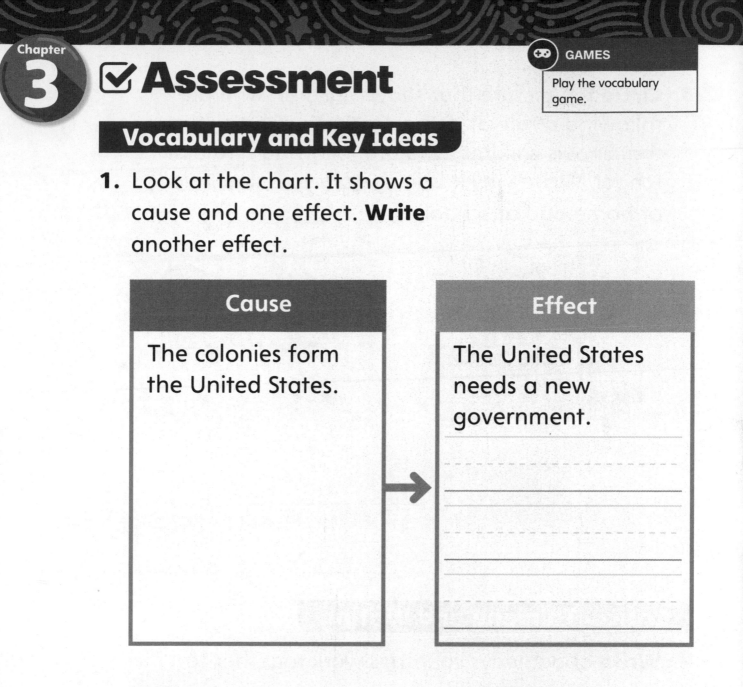

Cause	Effect
The colonies form the United States.	The United States needs a new government.

2. Write 1, 2, or 3 next to each step to tell how laws are made in the United States.

Ⓐ If the president says yes to the bill, it becomes law. _____

Ⓑ Both parts of Congress vote on a bill. _____

Ⓒ The bill is sent to the president if Congress agrees that it should be a law. _____

3. Circle the picture that shows children who are following a rule at home. **Underline** the picture that shows children who are following a rule at school. **Write** why it is important to follow rules at home and at school.

_____

_____

_____

_____

Critical Thinking and Writing

4. Write about ways countries work together to solve problems.

_____

_____

_____

_____

_____

_____

Quest Findings

INTERACTIVITY

Use this activity to help you prepare to write your skit and act it out.

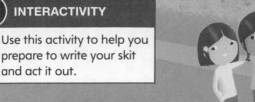

Write a Skit

It is time to put it all together. Write a skit and act it out!

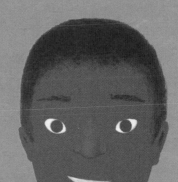

1 Plan Your Skit

Talk with a partner about rules we follow in school. Talk about what would happen if we did not have these rules. Then choose one rule you might try to do without.

2 Write Your Skit

Work with your partner to write your skit about different ways each person might act without this rule.

3 Practice Your Skit

Choose classmates to act out your skit. Have them practice your skit as you watch. Give them ideas to do it as you want.

4 Share Your Skit

Have your classmates act out your skit for the rest of the class. Or, if your teacher has the equipment, make a video of the skit. Then share it with the class.

People Who Supply Our Goods and Services

GO ONLINE FOR
DIGITAL RESOURCES

▶ VIDEO

👆 INTERACTIVITY

🔊 AUDIO

🎮 GAMES

☑ ASSESSMENT

📖 eTEXT

The **BIG** Question

How do people get what they need?

▶ VIDEO

Jumpstart Activity

👆 INTERACTIVITY

Look at where the family is shopping.
If you think they are shopping for needs, raise one hand.
If you think they are shopping for wants, raise two hands.
Draw a picture of a need here.

What We Buy

Preview the chapter **vocabulary** by singing the song to the tune of "Twinkle, Twinkle, Little Star."

We all **need** and **want** some things
For the uses that they bring.

All **producers** try and try
To make things we want to buy.

Workers make the **goods** so well
Add a price to make them sell.

Then they ship them to the store
For **consumers** to explore.

Choices like how much to pay
Take place at the stores each day.

A decision must be made,
Then the final bill gets paid.

Chapter 4

Quest
Writing Using Sources

Lend a Hand to Farmer Fran

Quest Kick Off

I'm Farmer Fran and I grow grapes, carrots, and artichokes. I don't have time to write an ad telling folks about my farm products. I want something fun. Can you do it for me?

1 Start with a Brainstorm

Pick one product and ask yourself questions to help you write the ad, such as *What is special about Farmer Fran's produce? How much will it cost?* Write down your ideas.

INTERACTIVITY

Learn more about Fran's farm and how an ad could help her.

2 Look for *Quest* Connections

Turn to the next page to begin looking for Quest connections that will help you write your ad.

3 Write Up Your *Quest* Findings

Use the Quest Findings page at the end of the chapter to help you write your ad.

Unlock The BIG Question

I will know the difference between a need and a want.

👆 INTERACTIVITY

Participate in a class discussion to preview the content of this lesson.

Vocabulary

needs
wants
choice
scarce
barter

Academic Vocabulary

purchase

JumpStart Activity

Take turns with a partner. Ask questions to guess something you each would like to have.

Needs and Wants

Needs are things we must have to live every day. Food, water, and clothing are needs. Shelter is also a need. A shelter is a place to live.

Wants are things that we would like to have, but we do not need them to live. Games, computers, Smartphones, and toys are wants. These things are fun to have. But they are not things we must have to live.

1. ☑ **Reading Check** Circle what needs are. **Underline** what wants are.

Getting What We Need and Want

There are many ways to get the things we need and want. Long ago, many people grew their food, made their clothing, and built their shelter. They met other needs through **barter.** Barter means trading one thing for another. A farmer would barter crops for supplies. A carpenter would make furniture and trade it for food or clothing.

Some people still grow their own food and make their own clothes. But most people today use money to buy food and clothing. They can go to stores. They can also use a computer to order and pay for things.

2. **☑Reading Check Circle two ways that people today can meet their needs.**

Making Choices

Quest Connection

Describe choosing a piece of fruit to eat.

INTERACTIVITY

Learn more about how we make choices.

Academic Vocabulary

purchase • to use money to pay for something

A **choice** is two or more things that we can pick or choose from. We can choose what we buy, or **purchase**. We can also choose the place or business where we will buy it.

There is another reason we make choices. We cannot have everything we want. This is usually because money is **scarce** or limited. We must choose what we can have and leave what we cannot have.

Families take care of their needs first. They choose the food and clothing they can buy and where they can live and work. They can make choices about what they want with money that is left.

3. ☑ **Reading Check** Cause and Effect **Look** at the picture. **Write** why a coat can be a need and a want.

_____

_____

_____

_____

_____

_____

Lesson 1 Check

INTERACTIVITY

Check your understanding of the key ideas of this lesson.

4. **Cause and Effect Underline** why we cannot buy everything we want.

5. How do we use money to choose what we need and want?

6. **Quest Connections** Write words for an ad to make a food the best choice to eat.

Analyze Costs and Benefits

Maria gets some money as a birthday gift. She must make a choice. She will either buy a zoo ticket or a board game.

Maria looks at the cost and benefits of each item. The **cost** is the money or price of something. The cost is also what you might have to give up or the work it takes. The **benefit** is the good result from a choice.

Cost: $20

Benefits: I can learn about animals. I can see the baby panda that was just born.

Maria decides to buy the zoo ticket. It costs more than the game. But she will learn a lot about animals. She can also see the baby panda before it grows up.

Your Turn!

1. **Read** the benefits and the cost of each item. **Mark** an X in the box for the item you would choose.

👆 **INTERACTIVITY**

Review and practice what you learned about costs and benefits.

What Will You Choose?

Item	Benefits	Cost	Choice
Ticket to 3-D dinosaur movie	1. Exciting to watch 2. Learn facts about dinosaurs	$12	☐
Soccer ball	1. Practice sports at home 2. Can use for many years	$18	☐

2. Why did you make this choice?

_____

_____

_____

_____

**Unlock
The BIG
Question**

I will know farmers use the land to produce food.

INTERACTIVITY

Participate in a class discussion to preview the content of this lesson.

Vocabulary

producers
harvest

Academic Vocabulary

natural

JumpStart Activity

Name your favorite fruit or vegetable. Draw a picture showing where you think it comes from.

Who Are Producers?

Producers are people who make or grow the things that other people need and want. Producers make the furniture, dishes, and clothes people use. They build the homes where people live.

Other producers make food for people to buy and eat. Bakers make bread. Cooks prepare soups. Cheesemakers produce cheese and yogurt.

1. ☑ **Reading Check** Use Evidence from Text **Underline** two things that producers make for people to eat.

The Role of Farmers

Farmers produce most food that people buy in stores. Some farmers grow fruits and vegetables like tomatoes, lettuce, and strawberries. Other farmers raise chickens for meat and eggs. Others raise dairy cows for milk.

Farms in the past were usually small. Farmers had horses or oxen to help them plant crops. Many farms today are still small, but some are large. Farmers now use big machines. These help them do their work.

2. ☑ **Reading Check** **Look** at the picture. **Draw an X** on the food in the field. **Circle the name of the food in the text.**

Word Wise

Highlight a word that means the same as *large*. **Underline** a word that means the opposite.

Quest Connection

Describe the kind of work done on a farm.

INTERACTIVITY

Learn more about farm work.

Academic Vocabulary

natural • from nature; not made by people

Planting and Harvesting

Farmers need resources, or supplies, to produce food. **Natural** resources are air, sunlight, water, and soil. Capital resources are money and tools such as tractors. Human resources are workers who **harvest** or pick the crops.

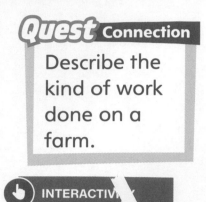

Different crops grow best at different times of the year. Some crops need more land or water than others to grow well. Some crops such as strawberries must be quickly harvested when they are ripe. Then the food will be fresh in the stores for people to buy. Other crops last longer and can be stored.

3. ☑ **Reading Check** **Look** at the picture. **Circle** a natural resource. **Draw an X** on a capital resource. **Draw a box** around a human resource.

☑ **Lesson 2 Check**

INTERACTIVITY

Check your understanding of the key ideas of this lesson.

4. **Main Idea and Details** Underline the three kinds of resources farmers need.

5. Why are farmers important producers?

_____

_____

_____

6. **Quest Connections** Think about the work farmers do. What can you say in your ad about Farmer Fran's fruit and vegetables?

_____

_____

_____

Identify Main Idea and Details

When you read a paragraph or listen to someone speak, look and listen for the main idea and details. The main idea tells you what the information is about. Details tell you more about the main idea.

Read the paragraph below. The main idea is circled. The details are underlined.

Long ago, farmers had few tools to help them. Plowing a field took a long time with a plow pulled by horses. Most farms were small. Many workers were needed to harvest and store the crops in a barn.

Your Turn!

1. **Read** the paragraph. **Circle** the main idea. **Underline** the details.

👆 INTERACTIVITY

Review and practice what you learned about how to identify a main idea and details.

Today, farmers have machines to help them plow the land and harvest crops. Farms do not need as many workers as they did in the past. Farmers can also work faster. They can farm larger areas of land than they used to.

2. **Compare** both paragraphs. **Write** a sentence that tells an important detail about how farming has changed.

_____

_____

_____

_____

Producing and Consuming Goods

Unlock The BIG Question

I will know how producers and consumers work together.

INTERACTIVITY

Participate in a class discussion to preview the content of this lesson.

Vocabulary

goods
consumers
services
process
distributors
markets

Academic Vocabulary

sequence

JumpStart Activity

Work with a partner. Write or draw how you would deliver a farmer's fresh produce in the quickest way possible.

Who Are Consumers?

Goods are things we need or want that producers make or grow. Producers sell goods in exchange for money. **Consumers** are people who buy and use goods and services. When you buy something, you are a consumer too! **Services** are the work done to help others. Doctors and store clerks provide services. So do community and government workers, like police and firefighters.

Producers can also be consumers. A cook buys many kinds of food to prepare in a restaurant. People who come to the restaurant buy and eat the food made by the cook.

From Farm to Market

Farmers grow and supply the food we eat. To get their goods to consumers, farmers need help from many people. These people do special jobs.

One job is to **process** food. These workers prepare the food to be sold. Another job is done by **distributors**, workers who sell and deliver food to the **markets**. These markets may be grocery stores or even bakeries. Finally, workers at the markets sell the food to consumers.

Long ago, most food was processed and distributed near farms. Consumers bought food locally. Then as roads crossed the nation and people began to freeze foods, these jobs could be done further away.

1. ☑ **Reading Check** **Highlight** what workers do to get a farmer's goods to market.

Quest Connection

How can the promise of a quick delivery help to sell a farmer's goods?

👆 **INTERACTIVITY**

Explore what farmers do to keep crops fresh.

Academic Vocabulary

sequence • the order in which events happen

How does a farmer's crop get from the farm to a market? You can see the order or **sequence** of steps in a flowchart.

How We Get Strawberries

1 Producers grow and harvest the strawberries.

⬇

2 Strawberries are packed and taken to coolers.

⬇

3 Crates are loaded on refrigerated trucks and delivered to markets.

FRESH STRAWBERRIES

⬇

4 Consumers buy strawberries.

2. ☑ **Reading Check** **Circle** the step where you can buy strawberries.

122

☑ Lesson 3 Check

3. Summarize How do producers and consumers work together?

_____

_____

_____

_____

_____

_____

4. Write one job workers do to help farmers sell their goods.

_____

_____

_____

_____

5. Understand the *Quest* **Connections Draw** pictures on the flowchart to show how consumers get fresh oranges from the farm.

Unlock The BIG Question

I will know how producers meet challenges.

INTERACTIVITY

Participate in a class discussion to preview the content of this lesson.

Vocabulary

weather
drought
climate
irrigation

Academic Vocabulary

source

JumpStart Activity

With a partner, act out one way weather can help or cause problems doing an activity outside.

Watching the Weather

Farmers want to grow good crops to earn money. It is important for farmers to watch the weather. **Weather** is what happens in the air at a certain place and time.

Bad weather can harm crops. Days may be too hot or cold. Strong winds or hail can shred plants. Frost can freeze and kill plants. Too much rain can drown plants. Not enough rain can cause a **drought**. The land dries up and plants die.

1. ☑ **Reading Check** **Highlight** two forms of weather that can hurt farmers' crops.

The Land and the Climate

Climate is the usual weather over a long time in one place. If the climate is warm and dry, farmers choose crops that grow well with little water.

Farmers also have to study the land. They look at water resources. They analyze the kind of soil. If farmers move to a new place, they have to learn about the land. They have to choose crops that will grow well and people will want to buy.

2. ☑ **Reading Check** **Main Idea and Details Write** two things a farmer should know before choosing crops.

_____

_____

Solving Problems

Farmers cannot control the weather. But they do have new and old ways to solve problems. If there is not enough rain, they can use **irrigation**. Irrigation brings water from a distant **source** to fields through pipes.

Lines of trees can be windbreaks. They keep strong winds from blowing away the soil. If there is a freeze, wind machines can keep air moving. Then ice will not form.

To stop harmful insects, farmers can use bugs that eat the insects but not the plants. They can also use plants that insects do not like to eat.

3. ☑Reading Check **Finish** the sentence. **When rain is scarce, farmers use**

_____

- -

_____ .

INTERACTIVITY

Check your understanding of the key ideas of this lesson.

☑Lesson 4 Check

4. **Cause and Effect** Why do farmers need to watch the weather?

_____

- -

_____

- -

_____

5. **Underline** three ways farmers solve problems caused by the weather.

6. **Tell** a partner what you would look for before starting a farm.

Photograph: Dairy Farm

You've learned about the different resources that are needed to produce goods and services. There are natural, capital, and human resources.

Dairy farmers are producers. They raise cows to produce milk. Suppose you want to know what resources a farmer needs to raise cows.

The photograph below is a primary source that can help you know what is needed. Look carefully at the photograph. What does it show? Take turns asking each other questions about the picture.

Primary Source

Using a Primary Source

Look at the photograph to answer these questions.

1. What are some natural resources a farmer needs to raise cows?

_____

- -

_____

2. What are some capital resources a farmer needs to raise cows?

_____

- -

_____

3. Based on this photograph, what can you write about the size of a dairy farm?

_____

- -

_____

- -

_____

Wrap It Up

Summarize what you learned about the resources a dairy farmer needs to raise cows.

_____

- -

_____

- -

_____

Quality:
Respect for the rights of others

Dolores Huerta
Champion for Farm Workers

Did you ever stand up for someone who was picked on? How did it feel to face the bully?

There are many people who show the courage to stand up for others. One person like that was Dolores Huerta. She stood up for the people who picked the fruits and vegetables in California fields. She believed these producers deserved to be treated fairly. She worked to make sure they got fair pay and healthier working conditions. Other people tried to stop her, but Huerta kept going until things got better.

How did Huerta try to improve her community?

_____

_____

_____

_____

_____

Survey Your Friends

Identify three things you can do to help people in your community. Survey friends to help you make a choice.

Vocabulary and Key ideas

1. **Fill in** the circle next to the best answer. What is the most common way people get their needs today?

(A) They grow or make what they need.

(B) They trade for what they need.

(C) They use money to buy what they need.

(D) They barter for what they need.

2. Think about how food moves from producers to consumers. What is the sequence of steps?

_____

_____

_____

_____

_____

_____

_____

_____

Critical Thinking and Writing

1. An orange farmer has limited resources. Should he buy a machine to pick oranges or have workers pick them? **Look** at the chart. **Mark** an X on what you would choose to do.

What Should We Choose?

Activity	Benefits	Cost	Choice
Pick with a machine 	1. Can harvest a lot of fruit quickly 2. Easier than picking by hand	Costs a lot of money	☐
Pick by hand	1. Fruit handled carefully 2. Saves money	Costs time and effort	☐

2. **Write** how the climate helps farmers choose which crops to plant.

_____

_____

_____

_____

_____

_____

Quest Findings

⏱ **INTERACTIVITY**
Learn about what makes a great ad.

Write Your Ad

It is time to put it all together and write your ad!

1 Prepare to Write

What kind of ad do you want? A splashy newspaper ad? How about a musical TV commercial? Remember, you want people to buy your good.

2 Write a Draft

Tell these details about your good: what it is, why people would like it, where they can buy it.

3 Share with a Partner

Tell each other ways to make your drafts better.

4 Revise Your Draft

Make changes to your ad. Check the words you used to describe your good.

5 Present Your Ad!

Draw a picture to go with your ad. Then show the class your ad. If you wrote a song, perform it for the class.

Carrots Give Me Energy!

Making a Difference

GO ONLINE FOR
DIGITAL RESOURCES

▶ VIDEO

👆 INTERACTIVITY

🔊 AUDIO

🎮 GAMES

☑ ASSESSMENT

📖 eTEXT

The BIG Question

What makes someone a hero?

▶ VIDEO

Jumpstart Activity

👆 INTERACTIVITY

Stand like a superhero you know from a book or movie. Act out your super power for a partner to guess what it is and how you use it.

🔊 AUDIO

Making a Difference

Preview the chapter **vocabulary** by singing the song to the tune of "This Old Man."

The **common good** in our country
is something good for you and me.
Justice means we're treated fair.
This is something we all share.

Courage, risk, and **sacrifice**
brought about our **civil rights.**
Experiments created **vaccines**
to help us all stay healthy.

Quest

Project-Based Learning

Help Honor Our Heroes

Quest Kick Off

I'm Super Storyteller. I'm using my super powers to write books about heroes. Can you help me draw the covers? Learn more about a hero. Then create a book cover that will make people want to learn about and honor your hero.

Start with a Brainstorm

Pick one hero. Ask yourself questions to get ideas for your cover. Here are some possible questions: What is special about my hero? What did he or she do that was heroic? Write down your ideas.

INTERACTIVITY

Think about what makes someone a hero and why we honor heroes.

---

2 Collect Clues for *Quest* Connections

Turn to the next page to begin looking for your Quest Connections.

CERTIFICATE OF EXCELLENCE

---

3 Draw Your Book Cover

Quest Findings

At the end of the chapter, use what you learned to draw your book cover.

1 What Makes a Hero?

I will know what makes someone a hero.

> 👆 **INTERACTIVITY**
>
> Participate in a class discussion to preview the content of this lesson.

Vocabulary

trait
courage
risk
sacrifice
common
 good

Academic Vocabulary

goal

JumPstart Activity

Work with a partner. Talk about something you did that was helpful but also hard to do.

Who Is a Hero?

There are heroes in books and movies. In real life, you do not need to wear a mask or cape. You do not need a super power to be a hero.

A hero can be anyone who works hard to help others. Heroes share important traits. A **trait** is something special about a person. Traits include being kind and hard working. Heroes know right from wrong. Heroes are often brave, or have **courage**, too.

1. ☑ **Reading Check** **Underline** four traits shared by most heroes.

How Does a Hero Act?

Heroes behave in special ways. They are ready to act when others are not. They will take a risk to help others. A **risk** is the chance that something bad might happen.

Heroes keep trying even when others have failed. They love and support their community and country. They tell the truth.

Heroes often make sacrifices. A **sacrifice** is something you give up to help someone else. A hero puts the needs of others first.

2. ☑**Reading Check** **Write about one of the heroes you see in the pictures. Tell what the person is doing that makes him or her a hero.**

_____

_____

_____

_____

Why Does a Hero Act?

Word Wise

Antonyms
Many people know about a *famous* person.
Highlight a word that means the opposite of *famous*.

Heroes do not set out to be heroes. They are regular people who are moved to do amazing things. They are thinking about the common good. The **common good** is something that is good for all people. They are not looking to get famous. They are not thinking about making money.

3. ☑**Reading Check** Compare and Contrast Mark an X in the box for the heroic act. Talk with a partner about your answer.

	Rode home fastest on a bicycle	☐
	Saved a kitten from a fire	☐

Why Are Heroes Important?

The actions of heroes in the past make our world better today. We look up to them, and they make us want to help each other. They teach us to never give up on our **goals**.

Academic Vocabulary

goal • something that you are trying to reach

INTERACTIVITY

Check your understanding of the key ideas of this lesson.

☑ Lesson 1 Check

4. **Main Idea and Details Look** at the photo. Talk with a partner about traits and actions that make this person heroic.

5. **Draw** a person doing something heroic.

6. **Write** about something that might happen that would cause someone to act like a hero.

_____

_____

_____

_____

I will know about heroes who were leaders.

> 👆 **INTERACTIVITY**
>
> Participate in a class discussion to preview the content of this lesson.

Vocabulary

inspire
justice
Civil War
reservation

Academic Vocabulary

behalf

JumpStart Activity

Play a game of follow the leader with friends. Take turns being the leader.

Heroes Know How to Lead

Leaders are able to get people to follow them. Some leaders use words to spread their ideas. They write papers and give speeches. Others use action to move, or **inspire**, people. They lead marches and fight battles.

Some leaders become heroes. These leaders make a difference in the lives of others. Their ideas and actions change the world for the better.

1. ✅ **Reading Check** Compare and Contrast Tell a partner about the different ways leaders get people to follow them.

Abraham Lincoln

Abraham Lincoln was the 16th President of the United States. As a young boy, he was poor. He liked to read books and tell stories. He became a lawyer. He gave many speeches about justice. **Justice** is a fair way of treating all people.

Abraham Lincoln was the leader during a war between the states in our country. This war is called the **Civil War**. The states were fighting for many reasons. One reason was because some states wanted African Americans to be free but other states did not. Abraham Lincoln worked hard to keep our country together. He knew it was wrong for African Americans not to be free. He took actions to free them and inspired others to do the same.

2. ☑ **Reading Check** Use Evidence from the Text **Underline** two reasons why Abraham Lincoln is a hero.

Sitting Bull

Sitting Bull was a leader of the Sioux nation. The Sioux nation is a group of American Indian tribes. They live in the North American Great Plains.

Sitting Bull became known for his courage as a young man. At the Battle of Little Bighorn in 1876, he led his people to victory over U.S. troops. The Sioux nation wanted the right to live freely on their land. But they soon ran out of food and became too hungry to fight. They were forced to live on a **reservation**, or an area of land set aside for the American Indians.

Sitting Bull became a hero. Many people came to meet him. They respected him. They liked the way he worked on **behalf** of his people for their rights.

3. ☑ Reading Check **Complete the sentence. Sitting Bull is a hero because**

_____

_____

_____

_____

Academic Vocabulary

behalf • for other people's benefit

Golda Meir

Golda Meir was one of Israel's leaders. Israel is in the Middle East. It became a country in 1948. She believed in Israel's independence. But some countries' leaders did not, and they fought in wars against Israel. Golda Meir worked hard for peace and to gain support for Israel.

👆 INTERACTIVITY

Check your understanding of the key ideas of this lesson.

☑ Lesson 2 Check

4. **Compare and Contrast Write** about how Golda Meir and Sitting Bull are alike.

_____

_____

_____

_____

5. **Identify** the event that happened while Lincoln was president. What action did he take?

_____

_____

_____

_____

6. Talk with a partner about why some leaders become heroes.

Lesson 3

Heroes Who Inspire Change

Unlock The BIG Question

I will know about heroes who inspire change.

INTERACTIVITY

Participate in a class discussion to preview the content of this lesson.

Vocabulary

civil rights
protest
race
boycott

Academic Vocabulary

considerable

JumPstart Activity

Work with a partner. Draw peaceful ways you can get other people to listen to you.

Heroes Work for Justice

You know that Abraham Lincoln worked for justice. Other people did too. They wanted to make sure that everyone was being treated the same. They worked for **civil rights**, or equal treatment under the law.

Harriet Tubman lived during the 1800s. She wanted to help other African Americans who were not free. They were treated badly and had no rights. Harriet Tubman led many of these African Americans to freedom on a secret path called the Underground Railroad.

Martin Luther King, Jr.

Dr. Martin Luther King, Jr. led protest marches for equal rights for African Americans during the 1960s. To **protest** means to speak strongly against something. Dr. King's actions helped lead to the Civil Rights Act of 1964. This law said that all people must have the same opportunities. Dr. King inspired people to work peacefully for their civil rights.

Others worked for civil rights, too. Yuri Kochiyama gave speeches protesting treatment of Japanese Americans and people of other races. **Race** is a trait shared by a group of people. Wilma Rudolph was one of the world's fastest runners in 1960. She fought hard to try to make women's sports equal to men's.

1. ✓ **Reading Check** **Underline** what Dr. King's actions led to and what he inspired others to do.

Harriet Tubman

Yuri Kochiyama

Wilma Rudolph

Heroes of Women's Rights

Today, girls and boys go to school together. They can work hard and become whatever they want to be. In the past, there were **considerable** limits on what girls could do. Girls were not allowed to go to the same schools as boys. Women were not allowed to have the same jobs as men.

Women also were not allowed to vote to change these unfair rules. Women held protests and gave speeches. By 1920, women gained the right to vote.

But women were still not treated the same as men. People continued to speak out. Betty Friedan was an author who wrote an important book in 1963. In it, she encouraged women to fight for their rights and for better treatment.

Academic Vocabulary

considerable •
large in number

Her book inspired other women to join the fight. They worked with government leaders. They asked for unfair laws to change.

Bella Abzug was a lawyer who fought for equal rights. She wanted equal pay for men and women. She was elected to Congress in the 1970s.

Gloria Steinem worked on behalf of women's issues too. She worked with other female leaders to change how women were treated. She also started a magazine for women and wrote books on women's rights.

Quest Connection

Describe some women's rights heroes and actions taken by them.

INTERACTIVITY

Think about the actions women took to try to gain equal rights. Talk with a partner about why women worked hard to gain equal rights.

2. ☑ **Reading Check** Draw Conclusions **Look at the two photos that show groups of women. Talk with a partner about what is happening in each one. What can you tell from these pictures about the fight for women's rights?**

Heroes of Workers' Rights

Other heroes helped workers. In the late 1800s, many people worked long hours in dangerous conditions. Samuel Gompers, an immigrant from England, wanted workers to be treated more fairly. He worked to get people higher wages and better working conditions.

César Chávez and Dolores Huerta were heroes of farm workers. They fought to make the lives of these workers better. They saw the poor way these immigrants from Mexico and other Latin American countries were treated.

Chávez and Huerta joined together and began the National Farm Workers Association. It later became the United Farm Workers. These leaders were able to get workers and consumers across the country to take part in a peaceful **boycott**. Millions of people stopped buying or using some products in support of farm workers. Then laws were changed. Chávez and Huerta had gotten more rights and more money for farm workers.

3. ☑ Reading Check **Underline the group César Chávez and Dolores Huerta started and what it became.**

✅ Lesson 3 Check

4. Summarize Write how Samuel Gompers made a difference in people's lives.

_____

_____

_____

_____

5. Choose a civil rights leader who inspires you. **Write** why the person inspires you.

_____

_____

_____

_____

_____

6. Understand the _Quest_ **Connections Draw** a leader of women's rights doing something heroic. Talk with a partner about what the person is doing.

Rosa Parks: *My Story*

During the 1950s and 1960s, many people protested against the unfair way African Americans were treated. Rosa Parks did this. Her actions made her a civil rights hero.

Rosa Parks

On December 1, 1955, Rosa Parks refused to give up her bus seat to a white person. This was the law at the time, so she was sent to jail. Her actions inspired many people. They held a bus boycott. Laws were changed so seating on buses became fair. Here is what Rosa Parks said about that day:

Vocabulary Support

tired in my body ·······

a picture of me in their minds ···

doing what I was told ·······

although, even though

People always say that I didn't give up my seat because I was tired, but that isn't true. I was not <u>tired physically</u>, or no more tired than I usually was at the end of a working day. I was not old, although some people have <u>an image of me</u> being old then, I was 42! No, the only tired I was, was tired of <u>giving in</u>.

– Rosa Parks: *My Story*

Using a Primary Source

1. Write what you think Rosa Parks meant when she said she was "tired of giving in."

_____

_____

_____

_____

2. Why do you think Rosa Parks is called a hero of civil rights?

_____

_____

_____

_____

Wrap It Up

Summarize how Rosa Parks' actions made a difference for African Americans and their civil rights.

_____

_____

_____

_____

_____

_____

I will know about heroes of science.

INTERACTIVITY

Participate in a class discussion to preview the content of this lesson.

Vocabulary

invention
element
vaccine
experiment

Academic Vocabulary

discovery

JumpStart Activity

Talk with a partner about some tasks you do every day. Then brainstorm something you could make so it would be easier, faster, or safer to do one of those tasks.

Thomas Edison's Ideas and Inventions

Thomas Edison was not afraid to ask questions and look for answers. He spent a lot of time taking things apart. That was how he learned how they worked. Then he started using his ideas to make inventions. An **invention** is something new. Edison made more than 1,000 inventions. He built a place where he could work on his inventions. Each invention came about because he saw a need to create or improve something. He worked on each one until it met that need.

One of Thomas Edison's first inventions was the phonograph. It is a machine that records the sound of a voice, then plays it back. The first words he recorded were "Mary Had a Little Lamb."

Thomas Edison also invented the electric light bulb. It let people work and play into the night. He came up with the idea of places that could make power too. From these places, or power plants, wires could bring power into people's homes.

Edison's work led to other people making inventions. These inventions include toasters, washing machines, and many other things we use today.

1. ☑ **Reading Check** **Talk to a partner about how electric power helps you.**

Ideas That Changed the World

Academic Vocabulary

discovery • the act of finding or learning something for the first time

Marie Curie and Albert Einstein were hard-working scientists who made important **discoveries**. Both were awarded the Nobel Prize for physics, a type of science.

Marie Curie discovered two **elements**, materials from which everything in the universe is made. Her findings help to treat cancer, a serious disease.

Albert Einstein received a compass when he was five years old. This made him curious about magnets and science. Later, Einstein used science and math to form ideas about how objects in space move. Other scientists took his ideas and made predictions about space. This led to more discoveries about space and planets.

Louis Pasteur was a French scientist who lived during the late 1800s. He made discoveries about germs. Germs can cause disease and food to spoil or go bad. He found ways to make milk and other foods safer. His tireless work in studying germs saved many lives. His determination helped keep farm animals safe and healthy.

Quest Connection

Describe ways scientists' discoveries affected the world.

2. ☑Reading Check **Compare and Contrast Draw a line from the scientist to how his or her idea affected the world.**

INTERACTIVITY

Talk with a partner about how some scientists' ideas have made people's lives better.

Marie Curie   People are able to eat safely.

Louis Pasteur   People with cancer are helped.

Albert Einstein   People discovered more about space and planets.

Heroic Discoveries in Medicine

American doctors Jonas Salk and Charles Drew made medical discoveries that saved many lives. Jonas Salk made a vaccine to fight polio, a disease that harmed young people. A **vaccine** can keep people safe from disease. The United States is now polio free. Charles Drew started blood banks where large amounts of blood can be stored for later use. Our bodies need healthy blood to stay alive.

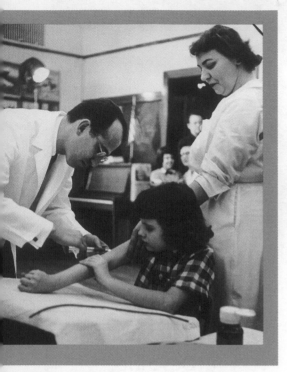

Jonas Salk

3. ☑ Reading Check **Compare and Contrast Ask and answer a question about how Jonas Salk's work is different from Charles Drew's work.**

A Hero in Space

Sally Ride showed courage as the first American woman to rocket into space. She trained as a pilot with NASA. NASA is a U.S. government group that studies and explores space.

Charles Drew

Sally Ride went on two space trips and did science experiments. An **experiment** is a test to prove a fact. She inspired girls to follow careers in science.

INTERACTIVITY

Check your understanding of the key ideas of this lesson.

☑ **Lesson 4 Check**

4. Main Idea and Details Write why Sally Ride is a hero. Talk with a partner about your answer.

_____

_____

_____

_____

5. Complete the sentence. My world might be different without Louis Pasteur because

_____

_____

_____

_____

6. Understand the Quest Connections **Choose a hero of science. List** some details about that person.

_____

_____

_____

Compare and Contrast

When you *compare*, you tell how two or more things are alike. When you *contrast*, you tell how they are different.

You can compare and contrast pictures and words. Look at the pictures. They are of two music players. The picture on the left is a phonograph. Thomas Edison invented it in 1877. The picture on the right shows a digital music player. It was invented in 2001.

Talk with a partner about how the two inventions are similar. Talk about how they are different.

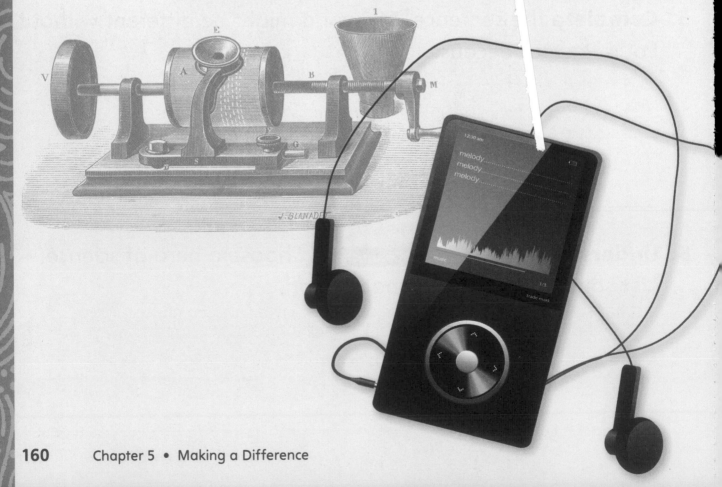

Your Turn!

1. **Read** the two paragraphs. Talk with a partner about how the paragraphs are alike and different.

INTERACTIVITY

Review and practice what you learned about comparing and contrasting.

Thomas Edison wanted to make a safe light bulb. In 1879, he did just that. It lasted for more than 14 hours. But only part of the energy made by the bulb was used for light. The rest went into the air as heat. So Edison's light bulb did not use energy in the best way.

Thomas Edison might be excited to learn about modern light bulbs. Today, most use more than 80 percent less energy than his. So they use energy wisely. They can last more than 25 times longer too. They are still safe to use.

2. **Underline** two ways today's light bulbs are different from Edison's light bulb. **Circle** one way today's light bulb is like Edison's.

Unlock
The**BIG**
Question

I will know about heroes who help people.

👆 **INTERACTIVITY**

Participate in a class discussion to preview the content of this lesson.

Vocabulary

poverty
volunteer

Academic Vocabulary

establish

JumpStart Activity

Work with a partner. Act out ways you can help people in your community

Heroes Help People

Some heroes are helpers. Helpers work with people who are in need of care, food, or housing. They help make lives better.

Jane Addams was an important helper. She spent her life helping families living in poverty. **Poverty** means very poor. She worked to change laws unfair to children, workers, and women. She spoke up for peace and against war.

1. ☑**Reading Check** **Underline** who Jane Addams spent her life helping. **Circle** what she spoke up for and against.

A House of Hope

Jane Addams rented a big house in Chicago, Illinois, in 1889. She asked immigrants to live there. The house was called Hull House. Today, Hull House is a museum.

Hull House offered many services. For example, children could get day care or go to school. Parents could learn English or get help finding jobs. Families could go to theater or music and art classes.

Jane Addams once said:

Primary Source

Nothing could be worse than the fear that one had given up too soon, and left one unexpended [not used up; remaining] effort that might have saved the world.
—Jane Addams

2. ☑ **Reading Check** **Write** a summary of Jane Addams' quote. Talk with a partner about why she is a hero.

_____

_____

_____

_____

_____

Quest Connection

Talk with a partner about why the earliest Red Cross workers were heroes.

INTERACTIVITY

Think about how the actions of a few people may make a difference for people of future generations.

Academic Vocabulary

establish • to begin

The Red Cross

The Red Cross is a group that helps lessen suffering. Red Cross groups are found around the world. They help people during times of war, peace, and emergencies. They find people shelter. They give out free water, food, and medicine.

Henri Dunant **established** the Red Cross in 1864 in Switzerland. He saw wounded soldiers after a battle. So Dunant organized volunteers to help the soldiers. A **volunteer** is someone who works for free.

Clara Barton was a nurse, and she organized the Red Cross in America. She helped soldiers during the Civil War.

3. ☑ **Reading Check** Cause and Effect **Talk** to a partner about the effect war had on Dunant and Barton.

The Mother of Nursing

Florence Nightingale is called the mother of nursing. She saw wounded soldiers die from poor care in the hospital during a war. So she bought new clothing and healthy food for them. She made sure everything was clean. Florence Nightingale started a school for nurses after the war.

INTERACTIVITY

Check your understanding of the key ideas of the lesson.

☑ Lesson 5 Check

4. **Main Idea and Details** Tell a partner why Florence Nightingale is called the mother of nursing.

5. **Write** a short newspaper advertisement for Hull House.

_____

_____

_____

_____

_____

6. **Understand the** Quest Connections **Draw** a picture of a hero from this lesson helping someone in need.

Analyze Images

Images include photographs, paintings, posters, and even videos. To find out what an image means, you analyze it. You look at it closely.

First, figure out who the image is for, or the audience. Then decide its purpose. Next, decide what is going on in the image.

Finally, see if the image creates a feeling. How might the woman be feeling? Think about how it makes you feel. Talk with a partner about these things.

People who need service dogs find out how helpful they can be.

Read the caption. It tells what is happening in the photo.

A dog helps a woman shop at the grocery store.

Look closely at the image below.

● INTERACTIVITY

Review and practice what you learned about analyzing images.

1. **Write** who you think this poster was for and what you think its purpose was.

_____

_____

_____

_____

_____

_____

_____

_____

_____

_____

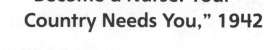

"Become a Nurse: Your Country Needs You," 1942

2. **Read** the caption. **Underline** when the image was made.

3. **Draw** an X on a detail of the image that makes you think of America.

4. Talk with a partner about how this image makes you feel. Tell why you feel that way.

How We Can Make a Difference

Unlock The BIG Question

I will know how I can make a difference.

INTERACTIVITY

Participate in a class discussion to preview the content of this lesson.

Vocabulary

first responder

Academic Vocabulary

ongoing

JumPstart Activity

Draw a picture of someone you know who likes to help other people. Label your picture.

Heroes Are All Around Us

You have read about famous heroes from long ago and the recent past. But many heroes are not famous. They live in our homes. They live in our community.

Think about your friends, family, and neighbors. Which of them are community heroes? Community heroes give and share their time and talents. They do these things for the common good.

1. **✓ Reading Check** **Details** **Underline** why community heroes share their time and talents.

Artists and Service Workers

Artists can be community heroes. An author or painter might direct his or her work on a community problem. A musician might hold a concert to help a community raise funds for a charity.

Service workers are community heroes. Many service workers are also volunteers. Some keep us safe. Soldiers are service workers. First responders are service workers, too. They save lives. **First responders** are police, firefighters, and Emergency Medical Teams. An Emergency Medical Team can have doctors, nurses, and ambulance drivers.

2. ☑ **Reading Check** Details
Circle the names of three kinds of service workers.

You Can Make a Difference

You can make a difference too. Think about some **ongoing** problems in your school or community. A problem might be littering or bullying. You and your class can work together to make a plan. People in your community might be able to help too. Then everyone can work as a team to solve the problem.

3. ✓ **Reading Check** **Fill out** the chart with your classmates. **Identify** a problem in your school or community. **Talk** about ways to solve it. **Vote** on a plan to solve it. Discuss the steps involved.

Solving a Community Problem

Problem	→	Solution

4. **Main Idea and Details** Who is a hero that you know? **Write** about how he or she makes a difference in your life.

_____

_____

_____

_____

5. **Draw** a picture of a service worker in your community. **Write** a caption for your picture.

6. Be a music hero. Work with a partner. **Write** a short song about a problem in your school or community. Use a separate sheet of paper. Then sing or record your song and play it for your class.

_____

_____

**Quality:
Determination**

Sequoyah
Maker of the Cherokee Writing System

Sequoyah was a Cherokee Indian. He admired how many Americans could communicate through writing. The Cherokee did not have a way to write their language. Sequoyah was determined to create something to help the Cherokee use writing to communicate. He made about 85 different characters that stood for different parts of Cherokee words. In doing so, he created a Cherokee writing system! It was soon used in the Cherokee Nation. Across the country, statues were built to honor him. Schools and other buildings were named after him, too.

Write about how Sequoyah's determination helped the Cherokee Nation.

Interview Your Family

Ask family members to describe a time when they were determined to do something.

☑ Assessment

🎮 GAMES

Play the vocabulary game.

Vocabulary and Key Ideas

1. **Fill in** the circle next to all the correct answers. Which **traits** do heroes often have?

   (A) courageous

   (B) fast

   (C) hard working

   (D) kind

2. **Look** at the names and pictures. **Circle** the person who is a hero of science. **Underline** the person who is a hero of civil rights. **Put** an X on the person who is a hero of women's rights.

   Bella Abzug

   Albert Einstein

   Rosa Parks

3. Compare and Contrast Why might Sitting Bull, Samuel Gompers, and César Chávez all be called heroic leaders?

_____
_____
_____
_____
_____
_____

Critical Thinking and Writing

4. Write why these community workers might be called heroes.

_____
_____
_____
_____
_____
_____
_____
_____
_____

Quest Findings

INTERACTIVITY

Use this activity to help you prepare to draw a book cover to honor a hero.

Draw a Book Cover

It is time to put it all together and draw your book cover.

1 Plan Your Book Cover

Which hero do you want to draw? Will it be a famous hero from long ago? How about a hero from your community? Remember, you want people to learn something about your hero.

2 Draw Your Book Cover

Draw your book cover. Show a key event from the person's life. Then write the hero's name. Also include a subtitle that explains why he or she is a hero.

3 Present Your Book Cover

Show your classmates your book cover. Tell them why you picked your hero.

Chapter 6
Our American Culture

GO ONLINE FOR
DIGITAL RESOURCES

▶ VIDEO

👆 INTERACTIVITY

🔊 AUDIO

🎮 GAMES

☑ ASSESSMENT

📖 eTEXT

The BIG Question

How is culture shared?

▶ VIDEO

Jumpstart Activity

👆 INTERACTIVITY

Stand up and go to the class map.
How many countries do you know?
Point and name them!

Sing About It!

◀) AUDIO

Festival Time

Preview the chapter **vocabulary** by singing the song to the tune of "Do Your Ears Hang Low?"

There's a **festival.**

Please come along with me.

We'll attend a **ceremony.**

There's a lot to do and see.

We can learn about our **culture.**

What a fun time it will be,

At the festival.

Amazing Artifacts

Quest Kick Off

Hello! I'm Tim the Traveler. I travel all over the world to learn about different cultures. Now I want to find out about your culture! Can you bring an artifact about your culture to class and teach me about it? Please make sure it is a primary source.

Look around you! You might see people who come from different places. There are many cultures in our community. People celebrate different holidays in our schools and neighborhoods.

People work together in communities across the country. Some people organize festivals to celebrate many different cultures at the same time. Other groups help each other learn the languages they speak. Culture brings people together. It **continues** to teach us about the world we live in.

1. ☑ Reading Check **Write about what makes your culture special. Think about the language, music, and celebrations.**

_____

- - - - - - - - - - - - - - - - - - -

_____

_____

- - - - - - - - - - - - - - - - - - -

_____

Quest Connection

What are some different musical instruments you have seen or heard?

INTERACTIVITY

Learn more about different music.

Academic Vocabulary

instrument • object used to make music

What Music We Play

Music is an important part of games, festivals, and celebrations. Songs can be fast or slow to make people feel differently. How do you feel when you hear a quick, lively song? You might feel excited and full of energy!

Every culture has its own music. Different **instruments** are used to make different sounds. The Sikh musicians in the picture are playing special instruments. The sound they make is unique to their culture. They learned to play the instruments from their parents. They teach their children to play, too.

2. ☑ **Reading Check** Look at the picture. Do you have similar instruments in your culture? **Tell** a partner about instruments you know.

Your Turn!

1. **Circle** the holiday you like better.

   Thanksgiving   **4th of July**

 **INTERACTIVITY**

Review and practice what you learned about comparing points of view.

2. Does your point of view match Lin's or Juan's? Or do you have a different favorite holiday? **Write** your point of view and give one reason for it. **Turn** and **talk** to a partner to compare your points of view.

   _____

   _____

   _____

   _____

   _____

3. **Write** about a time you and a family member had different points of view.

   _____

   _____

   _____

   _____

   _____

Unlock The BIG Question

I will know about different cultures in the United States.

INTERACTIVITY

Participate in a class discussion to preview the content of this lesson.

Vocabulary

unique
diverse
parade
settled

Academic Vocabulary

character

JumpStart Activity

Ask your classmates where their parents were born. Find the states or countries on a map.

Many Cultures, One Country

People came to the United States from all over the world. They brought their **unique**, or special, culture and heritage with them. Today, our country is very **diverse**. This means it is made up of many different cultures. People like to share their culture. They enjoy learning about different food, music, and celebrations.

1. ☑ **Reading Check** **Check** the true sentence.

[ ] People in America come from one place.

[ ] People in America come from many different places.

New York City, New York

Many Chinese Americans live in New York City. Some live in a unique neighborhood called Chinatown. There, many restaurants and shops sell Chinese food. People speak English and Chinese. Parents teach their children about Chinese culture.

Chinese New Year is a big festival in the city! Every year, Mei's parents help her and her brother make decorations for a **parade**. A parade is a march to celebrate a special event. Together, they create a big colorful dragon and carry it down the street. People watch the parade as they celebrate the new year.

Chinese people have celebrated this festival for generations. It is an important part of their heritage.

2. ☑ **Reading Check** How do *you* celebrate the new year? **Tell** a partner.

New York

San Antonio, Texas

Many Mexican Americans live in San Antonio, Texas. Pedro was born in Texas but his grandmother was born in Mexico. She speaks to him in Spanish and teaches him to cook traditional Mexican food. Pedro learns about his culture from her.

On May 5, 1862, the Mexican army beat the French army in Puebla, Mexico. Every year, people in San Antonio celebrate this event with food, music, and dancing. The holiday is called Cinco de Mayo.

Pedro and his family always join in the festival. It is part of their culture. The festival helps form the unique **character** of San Antonio.

Academic Vocabulary

character • qualities which make up something

San Antonio

3. **Reading Check** Compare How is Pedro's life similar to his grandmother's? *They both _____.*

New Orleans, Louisiana

People from many different cultures live in New Orleans, Louisiana. Long ago, immigrants **settled**, or moved, there from Europe, and enslaved people were brought from Africa. They brought their unique music with them. Over the years, the music mixed together. Today, we call this type of music jazz.

Jazz music is important to the culture here. It is played at baseball games and important events. Each year, there is a big festival in New Orleans with parades, music, and food. It is called Mardi Gras. Jazz musicians march down the street while people dance and have fun.

Alex's family has lived in New Orleans for generations. They join in the Mardi Gras parade every year. Alex's parents have passed down their love of jazz music to him.

Quest Connection

What traditional clothing have you seen at a festival or celebration?

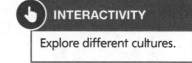

INTERACTIVITY

Explore different cultures.

St. Paul, Minnesota

Many Hmong live in St. Paul, Minnesota today. Paj was born here, but her parents came from Laos ten years ago. Paj's mother teaches her to cook traditional Hmong food. It is very spicy and delicious!

Every summer, there is a Hmong festival in St. Paul. People gather here to celebrate their culture. They sing and dance, eat traditional food, and play a game that is popular in their homeland. This game is similar to volleyball, but players cannot touch the ball with their hands.

Paj's father played this game in Laos. He is teaching Paj to play the game, too.

4. ☑ **Reading Check** **What game do you like to play? Did you learn it from your parents? Draw a picture of your favorite game.**

Together as One

America is made of immigrants from all over the world. They have each brought their own language, food, music, clothing, festivals, and traditions. Together, these cultures form the unique character of our country.

INTERACTIVITY

Check your understanding of the key ideas of this lesson.

☑ Lesson 2 Check

5. Choose a place you read about in this lesson. On another sheet of paper, **draw** a picture of what makes it unique.

6. **Compare and Contrast** Look at the pictures of the festivals and games in each city. **Write** how they are the same or different.

_____

_____

_____

_____

_____

_____

7. **Understand the Quest Connections Tell** a partner about clothing you have seen at a festival or celebration. **Describe** how the clothing looks and why it is important.

Unlock The BIG Question

I will know about American stories.

Vocabulary

fact
fiction
folk tale
tall tale

Academic Vocabulary

travel

JumpStart Activity

Play a game! Write two true things and one false thing about yourself. Read your sentences to the class. Who can guess which thing is false?

About American Stories

American stories are an important part of our heritage. These stories have been passed down for many generations, and are often told aloud. Some stories have **facts**. This means that parts are true. Some stories are **fiction**, which means that parts are made up.

A **folk tale** is a story which tells about the life of a real person. A **tall tale** tells about a person, too, but it is mostly fiction. A tall tale can start off with facts. Do not believe everything you hear, though!

1. ☑ **Reading Check** What is the difference between fact and fiction? **Tell** a partner.

John Henry

The story of John Henry is an American tall tale. In the story, John Henry is bigger and stronger than any man can be. The story goes like this ...

John Henry worked on the railroad. He was as tall as a giant! He carried a heavy hammer in each hand. He used the hammers to chip away at rock so that a big tunnel could be built. He was a mighty man! He built that tunnel all by himself.

👆 **INTERACTIVITY**

Check your understanding of the key ideas of this lesson.

☑ Lesson 3 Check

4. Ask and Answer Questions

Choose *fact* or *fiction* for each story.

	Mostly Fact	Mostly Fiction
1. "Why the Owl Has Big Eyes"	[ ]	[ ]
2. Johnny Appleseed	[ ]	[ ]
3. John Henry	[ ]	[ ]

5. Look at the story about John Henry. **Underline** a sentence that could be a fact. **Circle** a sentence that could not be a fact.

6. Tell a partner a story you know. Use sequence words to order the events. Have your partner decide if your story is fact or fiction and tell why.

Distinguish Fact from Fiction

A **fact** is something that is true. It can be proven. **Fiction** is not true. It can be made-up ideas. Sometimes fiction is based on facts.

Read the story about early cowboys. Some parts of the story are true and some parts are made up.

In the early 1800s, many cowboys lived in Texas. Some cowboys came from Mexico, while others were born in Texas. These cowboys raised cattle. One famous story tells about a Texas cowboy named Pecos Bill. Stories say he was the best cowboy who ever lived! Pecos Bill was raised by coyotes. He used a rattle snake as a lasso. One day, he rode a tornado. Other cowboys saw him bouncing and bucking. This is how they got the idea to ride horses in rodeos.

Look at the story. **Circle** a sentence that tells a fact. **Underline** two sentences that are fiction.

Your Turn! Activity

1. Look at the primary source below. It is a photo of a real cowboy doing his job. **Write** if it is fact or fiction. **Write** how the cowboy is similar to Pecos Bill. How is he different?

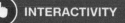
INTERACTIVITY

Review and practice what you learned about distinguishing fact from fiction.

_____

_____

_____

_____

_____

_____

_____

2. **Look** at the picture again. **Tell** a story about this cowboy. **Write** sentences with facts and fiction. Have a partner distinguish between the facts and fiction in your story.

Unlock The BIG Question

I will know why national holidays are important.

👆 **INTERACTIVITY**

Participate in a class discussion to preview the content of this lesson.

Vocabulary

honor
veteran
monument

Academic Vocabulary

treated

JumPstart Activity

Take a class poll. Which American holiday do your classmates like the best?

What We Celebrate

We have many special holidays. Some of these holidays **honor**, or celebrate, people. Weddings, birthdays, and graduations celebrate an important event in someone's life. Other holidays honor religious beliefs and traditions. These holidays include Christmas, Passover, Eid al-Fitr, Diwali, and Kwanzaa. We also honor our national heroes like Martin Luther King, Jr.

1. ☑ **Reading Check** Think about a holiday that you celebrate. **Tell** a partner what you do on that day.

Holidays for American Heroes

There are many heroes in our country. We remember them for their bravery or good deeds. We have two national holidays which honor the men and women who protect our country. On these days, people gather to watch parades. We listen to speeches, too.

Memorial Day is celebrated on the last Monday in May. On this special day, we remember all the United States citizens who died fighting for our country.

Veterans Day is celebrated in November. A **veteran** is a person who has served in the armed forces. On Veterans Day, we remember and honor all veterans. They fought to keep our country free.

2. ✓ Reading Check **Compare** How are **Memorial Day and Veterans Day similar? How are they different? Write** your answer.

_____

_____

_____

_____

_____

Celebrating Freedom

We honor the people who served as presidents of our country. George Washington led our country to independence. He later became the first president. Thomas Jefferson helped write the Declaration of Independence. Then he became the third president. Abraham Lincoln helped end slavery and the Civil War. Theodore Roosevelt wanted workers to be **treated** fairly. He also worked to conserve the land.

We celebrate Presidents' Day in February. We remember the heroes who helped shape our country. Another way we honor presidents is by building structures called **monuments**.

Academic Vocabulary

treated • behaved toward

3. ☑ Reading Check **Highlight** one president. **Underline** what makes him a hero.

Remembering a Hero for Justice

People in America didn't always have equal rights. Some groups were not treated fairly.

African Americans have been treated badly because of the color of their skin. Dr. Martin Luther King, Jr. believed that all Americans should have the same rights. He spoke out against unfair laws and helped change them. Dr. King gave a famous speech. He spoke about his dream that people would one day respect each other. We honor Martin Luther King, Jr. by celebrating his birthday every January.

Honoring Workers

Labor Day is celebrated on the first Monday in September. This holiday was created to honor workers and the contributions that they make every day to our country. People celebrate this holiday with parties, picnics, and even fireworks! People also honor workers' efforts by watching parades. The first Labor Day parade was held in New York on September 5, 1882. That day, about 10,000 workers took part in the parade.

4. ☑ Reading Check **Circle the reasons why people celebrate Martin Luther King, Jr. Day and Labor Day.**

☑ **Lesson 4 Check**

5. **Ask and Answer Questions Match** the holidays to who we honor. Write the letter on the line.

1. Memorial Day _____

2. Veterans Day _____

3. Presidents' Day _____

4. Martin Luther King, Jr. Day _____

5. Labor Day _____

a) heroes who were American presidents

b) a man who fought for African American rights

c) people who fought for our country

d) workers' contributions to our country

e) people who died fighting for our country

6. Choose one person we honor. **Write** what makes him a hero.

_____

_____

_____

_____

_____

7. Use separate paper. **Write** a list of holidays that you celebrate. **Draw** a picture that shows what you do for one of them.

Filipino American Traditional Dress

Traditional clothing is an important part of culture. In the Philippines, some men wear shirts and pants made of light material. It is hot in the Philippines! This type of clothing helps people stay cool.

A long time ago, Spanish people arrived in the Philippines. Spanish and Filipino culture mixed. People wanted to wear clothes that had a Spanish style.

Many Filipino Americans continue to wear traditional dress on special occasions. It is an important part of their culture today.

Shirts and pants move easily and are not tight against the body.

Filipino women began to wear a separate shirt and skirt instead of a dress, just like the Spanish.

Using a Primary Source

Answer these questions about traditional Filipino dress.

1. Look at the clothing in the pictures.
   Tell a partner about material and color.

2. **Highlight** the ways Filipino clothing is good for hot weather.

3. Based on these pictures, what can you **write** about Filipino culture?

_____

_____

_____

_____

Wrap It Up

Compare the clothing in the pictures to your clothing today. How does the weather affect what you wear? **Write** about it.

_____

_____

_____

_____

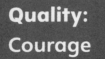

**Quality:
Courage**

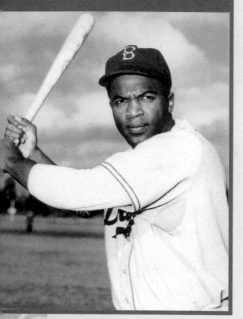

Jackie Robinson
Baseball Hero

Jackie Robinson was the first African American to play Major League Baseball. People did not want an African American to play baseball in the major leagues. They did not like the color of his skin. They threatened him and called him terrible names.

Jackie did not let these angry people stop him. He did not give up. He showed courage and stood up for his rights. He helped change people's minds. He helped get equal rights for all Americans.

Write about how Jackie showed courage.

_____

_____

_____

_____

_____

_____

_____

Talk About It

Turn and talk to a partner. **Tell** how you show courage.

☑ **Assessment**

Vocabulary and Key Ideas

1. **Main Ideas and Details Draw** your favorite festival and label the parts that show your culture. Use these words and your own ideas: *food, traditional clothing, music, dance.*

2. **Check** the correct answer. Why are traditional stories important to our culture?

[ ] They are always true.

[ ] They make us laugh.

[ ] They are passed down through generations.

3. **Distinguish Fact From Fiction Look** at the picture. **Circle** the sentence that is a fact about the picture. **Underline** the sentence that is fiction about the picture.

Everything-Maker pushed Owl's head into his body and pulled his ears straight up.

A story can be passed down orally for many generations.

Critical Thinking and Writing

4. Think about your older family members (grandparents, parents, aunts, and uncles). **Write** about how they have passed a holiday or other tradition from their culture on to you.

_____

_____

_____

_____

_____

_____

_____

Quest Findings

Show Off Your Artifact

It's time to put it all together and choose your artifact. Then show and tell!

INTERACTIVITY

Use this activity to help you prepare to share your artifact.

1 Prepare to Choose Your Artifact

Think about your culture. What holidays do you celebrate? What special clothing do you wear? Think about pictures or objects that you can share that represent your culture.

2 Research Your Artifact

Find out how your artifact represents your culture. What is it used for? How old is it? Where did it come from?

3 Take Notes About Your Artifact

Think about what your classmates might want to know about your artifact. Ask and answer questions about it.

4 Show and Tell!

Share your artifact with the class. Show off and celebrate your culture!

The United States of America, Political

Washington
★ Olympia

★ Salem

Oregon

Montana
★ Helena

North Dakota
★ Bismarck

South Dakota
Pierre ★

★ Boise
Idaho

Wyoming

Cheyenne ★

Nebraska

Lincoln ★

Carson City ★
Salt Lake City ★

Sacramento ★

Nevada

Utah

Denver ★
Colorado

Topeka ★
Kansas

California

Arizona
★ Phoenix

Santa Fe ★

New Mexico

Oklahoma
Oklahoma ★ City

PACIFIC OCEAN

Texas

★ Austin

Alaska

MEXICO

Juneau ★

★ Honolulu

Hawaii

CANADA

Minnesota

St. Paul
Wisconsin
Michigan
Madison
Lansing

Iowa
Des Moines

Indiana
Indianapolis

Springfield
Illinois

Jefferson
City
Missouri

Ohio
Columbus

New Hampshire
Vermont
Maine
Augusta
Montpelier
Concord
Albany
Massachusetts
New York
Boston
Hartford
Providence
Rhode Island
Connecticut
Pennsylvania
New Jersey
Harrisburg
Trenton
Annapolis
Dover
Delaware
Maryland
Washington, D.C.
Richmond
Virginia

West
Virginia
Charleston
Frankfort
Kentucky

Nashville
Tennessee

Raleigh
North
Carolina

Arkansas
Little
Rock

Alabama
Atlanta
Mississippi

Columbia
South
Carolina

ATLANTIC
OCEAN

Louisiana
Jackson
Montgomery
Georgia

Baton
Rouge
Tallahassee

Florida

Gulf of Mexico

N
W   E
S

Legend

⊛ National
capital

★ State
capital

Mt. Rainier ▲

Gannett Peak ▲

Rocky Mountains

▲ Mt. Elbert

Mt. Whitney ▲

PACIFIC OCEAN

MEXICO

Rio

Denali ▲

0   400 mi
0   400 km

0   100 mi
0   100 km

Maun
Kea

CANADA

Great
Lakes

Great Plains

Appalachian Mts.

ATLANTIC OCEAN

Grande

Gulf of Mexico

0   400 mi
0   400 km

N
W   E
S

Legend
Elevation
Feet   Meters

Feet	Meters
10,000	3,048
6,000	1,829
3,000	914
1,000	305
500	152
0	0

▲ Peak

R3

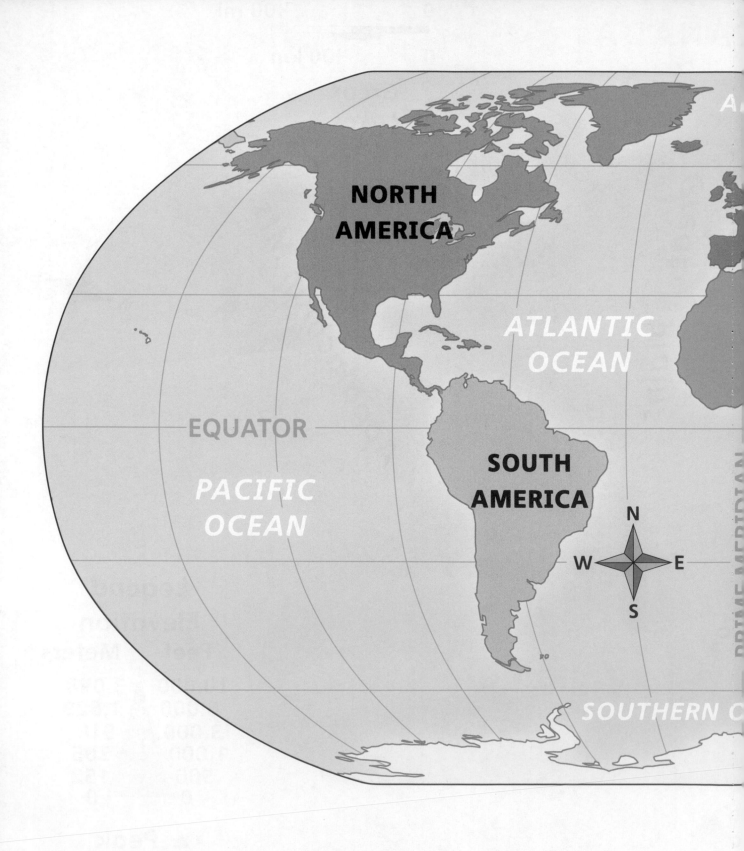

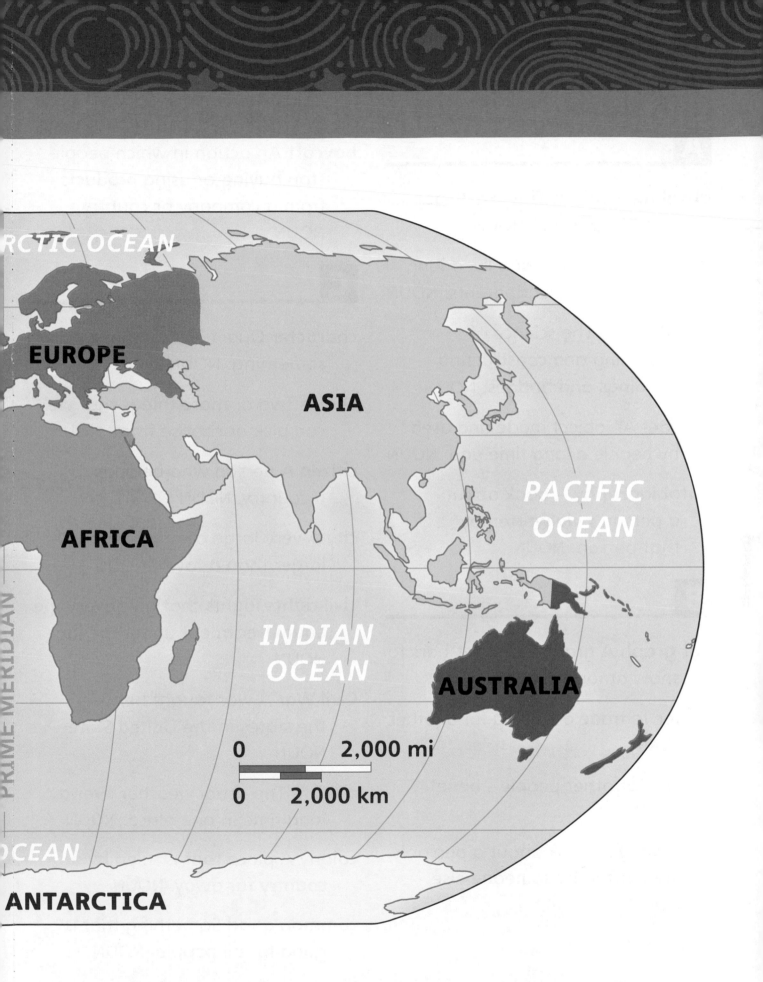

ARCTIC OCEAN

EUROPE

ASIA

AFRICA

PACIFIC
OCEAN

PRIME MERIDIAN

INDIAN
OCEAN

AUSTRALIA

0   2,000 mi

0   2,000 km

OCEAN

ANTARCTICA

Glossary

A

absolute location The exact spot where a place is. NOUN

ancestor A relative who lived long before your grandparents. NOUN

architecture The science of designing and constructing buildings and bridges. NOUN

artifact An object made and used by people a long time ago. NOUN

autobiography A book about a person's life written by that person. NOUN

B

bar graph A graph that uses bars to show amounts. NOUN

barter To trade one thing for another. VERB

behalf For other people's benefit. NOUN

biography A book about a person's life written by someone else. NOUN

boycott An action in which people stop buying or using products from a company or country. NOUN

C

character Qualities that make up something. NOUN

choice Two or more things that we can pick or choose from. NOUN

citizen A person who belongs to a country. NOUN

city A very large community, much larger than a town. NOUN

civil rights Rights that give everyone equal treatment under the law. NOUN

Civil War A war fought between the states in the United States. NOUN

climate The usual weather over a long time in one place. NOUN

colony A place that is ruled by a country far away. NOUN

common good Something that is good for all people. NOUN

community A place where people live, work, and play together; a group of people who share the same interests and beliefs. NOUN

compare To see how two or more things are similar. VERB

compass rose A symbol that shows directions on a map; also called a directional indicator. NOUN

conflict A serious disagreement. NOUN

Congress The part of government that writes and votes on laws. NOUN

consequence Something that happens as a result of an action. NOUN

considerable Large in number or amount. ADJECTIVE

constitution A plan for government that tells about a country's laws. NOUN

consumer A person who buys and uses goods and services. NOUN

continent A large land area on Earth. NOUN

continue To go on; not stop. VERB

contrast To see how two or more things are different. VERB

courage Bravery. NOUN

court A place where people decide if someone has broken a law. NOUN

culture A way of life. NOUN

D

discovery The act of finding or learning something for the first time. NOUN

distributor A person or company who sells goods to markets. NOUN

diverse From many different places. ADJECTIVE

document An official paper that supports something. NOUN

drought A long period when there is not enough rain; land dries up and plants die. NOUN

E

element A material from which everything in the universe is made. NOUN

environment The air, land, water, and life around us. NOUN

equator An imaginary line that divides Earth in half between the North Pole and the South Pole. NOUN

establish To set up. VERB

evidence Facts and information that are true. NOUN

examine To study something closely and carefully. VERB

experiment A test that is done to prove a fact. NOUN

extended family A family that includes more than parents and children, such as aunts and uncles. NOUN

 F

fact Something that can be proven. NOUN

family A group of people who live together and experience the world together. NOUN

family tree A drawing or diagram that shows how different family members are related to each other. NOUN

fiction Something that is not true. NOUN

first responder A police officer, firefighter, or EMT. NOUN

flow chart A drawing that shows how something works or how to do something. NOUN

folk tale A story that tells about a real person. NOUN

freedom The right to choose what we do and say. NOUN

G

generation People born and living about the same time. NOUN

geography The study of land, water, and people on Earth. NOUN

globe A round model of Earth. NOUN

goal Something you are trying to reach. NOUN

goods Things we need or want that producers make or grow. NOUN

government A group of people who work together to run a city, a state, or a country. NOUN

guardian A person who legally has the care of a person or the property of another. NOUN

H

harbor A safe place near land where ships are tied up. NOUN

harvest To pick crops. VERB

heritage A person's history and culture. NOUN

historian Someone who studies and writes about history. NOUN

history The story of the past. NOUN

honor To celebrate someone. VERB

I

immigrant A person who moves from one country to another country. NOUN

independence The state of being free from the rule of another government. NOUN

inspire To move people to think or do something. VERB

instrument Object used to make music. NOUN

interpret To make sense of or give meaning to. VERB

invention An original device. NOUN

irrigation The delivery of water from a distant source to fields through pipes. NOUN

J

journal A daily record of thoughts and events in a person's life. NOUN

justice Fair treatment for all. NOUN

L

landform The shape of Earth's land. NOUN

language Words that people use to communicate. NOUN

latitude Imaginary lines that run east and west around a globe. NOUN

law A rule we follow in our community, state, and country. NOUN

legend A box that identifies different symbols found on a map; also called a map key. NOUN

longitude Imaginary lines that run north to south on a globe, from the North Pole to the South Pole. NOUN

M

market A place where goods are sold. NOUN

migrate To move from one place to another. VERB

model A small object that stands for something much larger. NOUN

monument Something that is built to honor an important person or event in history. NOUN

N

natural From nature; not made by people. ADJECTIVE

need Something that we must have to live every day. NOUN

O

ocean A large body of salt water. NOUN

ongoing Continuing to happen. ADJECTIVE

oral history Recorded information from a person who experienced an event. NOUN

P

parade A march to celebrate a special event. NOUN

peace Freedom from fighting or war. NOUN

poverty The state of being very poor. NOUN

practice To follow teachings and rules. VERB

primary source Something written or made by a person who was part of or saw an event happen. NOUN

process To prepare or handle in a special way. VERB

producer A person who makes or grows the things that other people need and want. NOUN

protest To speak strongly against something. VERB

purchase To use money to pay for something. VERB

R

race A trait shared by a group of people. NOUN

relative location Tells where something is by comparing it to something else. NOUN

religion What a person believes in. NOUN

represent To speak for. VERB

reservation An area of land set aside for American Indians. NOUN

resource Something that people use. NOUN

respect High or special regard. NOUN

responsible Taking care of important things. ADJECTIVE

right Something we are free to do. NOUN

risk The chance that something bad might happen. NOUN

rural Describing an environment made up of small towns and farms. ADJECTIVE

S

sacrifice Something you give up to help someone else. NOUN

scale A measure of distance on a map. NOUN

scarce Limited. ADJECTIVE

secondary source Something written or made by someone who did not see or experience an event. NOUN

sequence The order in which events happen. NOUN

service Work done to help others. NOUN

settle To be in one place for a long time. VERB

source A place where something can be found. NOUN

suburb A community that is near a city. NOUN

Supreme Court The highest court in the United States. NOUN

symbol Something that stands for something else. NOUN

T

tall tale A story about a person with parts that are made up and hard to believe. NOUN

tax Money that is collected by government from its citizens. NOUN

town A small community. NOUN

trade To buy, sell, or exchange goods and services. VERB

tradition Something that is passed down over time. NOUN

trait Something special about a person. NOUN

travel To go from place to place. VERB

treated Behaved toward. VERB

U

unique Being the only one of something; special. ADJECTIVE

urban Describing a large community made up of a city and the places around it. ADJECTIVE

V

vaccine A product that protects people and animals from disease. NOUN

veteran A person who has served in the armed forces. NOUN

volunteer A person who works without pay. NOUN

vote To make a choice that can be counted. VERB

W

want Something that we would like to have but do not need to live. NOUN

weather What happens in the air at a certain place and time. NOUN

Glosario

A

absolute location/ubicación absoluta El punto exacto donde se encuentra algo. SUSTANTIVO

ancestor/ancestro Un pariente que vivió mucho antes que tus abuelos. SUSTANTIVO

architecture/arquitectura La ciencia de diseñar y construir edificios y puentes. SUSTANTIVO

artifact/artefacto Objeto hecho y usado por personas hace mucho tiempo. SUSTANTIVO

autobiography/autobiografía Libro acerca de la vida de una persona escrito por esa misma persona. SUSTANTIVO

B

bar graph/gráfica de barras Gráfica que usa barras para mostrar cantidades. SUSTANTIVO

barter/hacer un trueque Cambiarle una cosa por otra a alguien. VERBO

behalf/representación En beneficio de otras personas. SUSTANTIVO

biography/biografía Libro acerca de la vida de una persona escrito por otra persona. SUSTANTIVO

boycott/boicot Acción en la que personas dejan de comprar o usar productos de una empresa o un país. SUSTANTIVO

C

character/carácter Cualidades de algo. SUSTANTIVO

choice/elección Dos o más cosas entre las que podemos elegir. SUSTANTIVO

citizen/ciudadano Persona que pertenece a un país. SUSTANTIVO

city/ciudad Una comunidad muy grande, mucho mayor que un pueblo. SUSTANTIVO

civil rights/derechos civiles Derechos que dan a todos el mismo trato ante la ley. SUSTANTIVO

Civil War/Guerra Civil Guerra entre estados librada en los Estados Unidos. SUSTANTIVO

climate/clima El estado del tiempo habitual a lo largo del tiempo en un lugar. SUSTANTIVO

colony/colonia Un lugar que es gobernado por un país lejano. SUSTANTIVO

common good/bien común Algo que es bueno para todas las personas. SUSTANTIVO

community/comunidad Lugar donde las personas viven, trabajan y juegan juntas; un grupo de personas que comparten los mismos intereses y creencias. SUSTANTIVO

compare/comparar Ver en qué se parecen dos o más cosas. VERBO

compass rose/rosa de los vientos Símbolo que muestra direcciones en un mapa; también es llamado indicador direccional. SUSTANTIVO

conflict/conflicto Un desacuerdo serio. SUSTANTIVO

Congress/Congreso La parte del gobierno que escribe leyes y las vota. SUSTANTIVO

consequence/consecuencia Algo que ocurre como resultado de una acción. SUSTANTIVO

considerable/considerable En gran cantidad. ADJETIVO

constitution/constitución Plan de gobierno que indica las leyes de un país. SUSTANTIVO

consumer/consumidor Persona que compra y usa bienes y servicios. SUSTANTIVO

continent/continente Una gran área de suelo en la Tierra. SUSTANTIVO

continue/continuar Seguir; no detenerse. VERBO

contrast/contrastar Ver en qué se diferencian dos o más cosas. VERBO

courage/coraje Valentía. SUSTANTIVO

court/corte Lugar donde se decide si alguien no cumplió la ley. SUSTANTIVO

culture/cultura Un modo de vida. SUSTANTIVO

D

discovery/descubrimiento La acción de hallar o aprender algo por primera vez. SUSTANTIVO

distributor/distribuidor Persona o empresa que vende bienes a mercados. SUSTANTIVO

diverse/diverso De muchos lugares diferentes. ADJETIVO

document/documento Papel oficial que apoya algo. SUSTANTIVO

drought/sequía Periodo largo cuando no hay suficiente lluvia; la tierra se seca y las plantas mueren. SUSTANTIVO

E

element/elemento Material a partir del cual se forma todo lo que hay en el universo. SUSTANTIVO

environment/medio ambiente El aire, la tierra y el agua que nos rodean. SUSTANTIVO

equator/ecuador Línea imaginaria que divide a la Tierra por la mitad entre el Polo Norte y el Polo Sur. SUSTANTIVO

establish/fundar Crear. VERBO

evidence/evidencia Hechos e información que son ciertos. SUSTANTIVO

examine/examinar Estudiar algo de cerca y cuidadosamente. VERBO

experiment/experimento Prueba que se realiza para demostrar un hecho. SUSTANTIVO

extended family/familia extendida Familia que incluye más que padres e hijos, como por ejemplo tíos y tías. SUSTANTIVO

F

fact/hecho Algo que se puede demostrar. SUSTANTIVO

family/familia Grupo de personas que viven juntas y experimentan el mundo juntas. SUSTANTIVO

family tree/árbol genealógico
Dibujo o diagrama que muestra cómo están relacionados entre sí los miembros de una familia. SUSTANTIVO

fiction/ficción Algo que no es cierto. SUSTANTIVO

first responder/personal de emergencia Oficial de policía, bombero o paramédico. SUSTANTIVO

flow chart/diagrama de flujo
Dibujo que muestra cómo funciona algo o cómo hacer algo. SUSTANTIVO

folk tale/cuento folklórico Un relato acerca de una persona real. SUSTANTIVO

freedom/libertad El derecho de elegir lo que uno hace y dice. SUSTANTIVO

G

generation/generación Personas que nacieron y viven aproximadamente al mismo tiempo. SUSTANTIVO

geography/geografía El estudio del suelo, el agua y las personas en la Tierra. SUSTANTIVO

globe/globo terráqueo Modelo de la Tierra con forma de esfera. SUSTANTIVO

goal/meta Algo que intentas alcanzar. SUSTANTIVO

goods/bienes Cosas que necesitamos o queremos y los productores hacen o cultivan. SUSTANTIVO

government/gobierno Grupo de personas que trabajan juntas para hacer funcionar una ciudad, un estado o un país. SUSTANTIVO

guardian/tutor Persona que está legalmente a cargo de una persona o la propiedad de otra persona. SUSTANTIVO

H

harbor/puerto Lugar seguro cerca de la tierra donde se atan los barcos. SUSTANTIVO

harvest/cosechar Recoger los cultivos. VERBO

heritage/herencia Historia y cultura de una persona. SUSTANTIVO

historian/historiador Persona que estudia la historia y escribe sobre ella. SUSTANTIVO

history/historia El relato de lo que sucedió en el pasado. SUSTANTIVO

honor/honrar Homenajear a alguien. VERBO

I

immigrant/inmigrante Persona que pasa de vivir en un país a vivir en otro país. SUSTANTIVO

independence/independencia El estado de ser libre del control de otro gobierno. SUSTANTIVO

inspire/inspirar Hacer que las personas piensen o hagan algo. VERBO

instrument/instrumento Objeto usado para hacer música. SUSTANTIVO

interpret/interpretar Encontrar el sentido de algo o darle significado. VERBO

invention/invento Un artefacto original. SUSTANTIVO

irrigation/irrigación Envío de agua desde una fuente distante a los campos por medio de tuberías. SUSTANTIVO

J

journal/diario Anotaciones diarias de pensamientos y sucesos de la vida de una persona. SUSTANTIVO

justice/justicia Trato justo para todos. SUSTANTIVO

L

landform/accidente geográfico La forma de la tierra de nuestro planeta. SUSTANTIVO

language/idioma Palabras que las personas usan para comunicarse. SUSTANTIVO

latitude/latitud Líneas imaginarias que corren de este a oeste en un globo terráqueo. SUSTANTIVO

law/ley Regla que seguimos en nuestra comunidad, estado o país. SUSTANTIVO

legend/leyenda Una caja que identifica los diferentes símbolos que hay en un mapa. SUSTANTIVO

longitude/longitud Líneas imaginarias que corren de norte a sur en un globo terráqueo, desde el Polo Norte al Polo Sur. SUSTANTIVO

M

market/mercado Lugar donde se venden bienes. SUSTANTIVO

migrate/migrar Pasar de un lugar a otro lugar. VERBO

model/modelo Objeto pequeño que representa un objeto mucho más grande. SUSTANTIVO

monument/monumento Algo que se construye como homenaje a una persona importante o un suceso histórico. SUSTANTIVO

N

natural/natural De la naturaleza; no hecho por personas. ADJETIVO

need/necesidad Algo que debemos tener todos los días para vivir. SUSTANTIVO

O

ocean/océano Gran masa de agua salada. SUSTANTIVO

ongoing/constante Que ocurre todo el tiempo. ADJETIVO

oral history/historia oral Información transmitida por una persona que estuvo en un suceso. SUSTANTIVO

P

parade/desfile Marcha para celebrar un evento especial. SUSTANTIVO

peace/paz Libertad de no pelear o entrar en guerra. SUSTANTIVO

poverty/pobreza La situación de ser muy pobre. SUSTANTIVO

practice/practicar Seguir enseñanzas y reglas. VERBO

primary source/fuente primaria Algo escrito o hecho por una persona que fue parte de un suceso o lo vio ocurrir. SUSTANTIVO

process/procesar Preparar o manejar de una manera especial. VERBO

producer/productor Persona que elabora o cultiva las cosas que otras personas necesitan o quieren. SUSTANTIVO

protest/protestar Hablar para mostrar que uno está muy en contra de algo. VERBO

purchase/comprar Usar dinero para pagar algo. VERBO

R

race/raza Característica compartida por un grupo de personas. SUSTANTIVO

relative location/ubicación absoluta Decir dónde está algo en comparación con otra cosa. SUSTANTIVO

religion/religión Lo que una persona cree. SUSTANTIVO

represent/representar Hablar por alguien. VERBO

reservation/reserva Área de tierra reservada para indígenas norteamericanos. SUSTANTIVO

resource/recurso Algo que usan las personas. SUSTANTIVO

respect/respeto Estima muy alta o especial. SUSTANTIVO

responsible/responsable Que se ocupa de cosas importantes. ADJETIVO

right/derecho Algo que somos libres de hacer. SUSTANTIVO

risk/riesgo La posibilidad de que ocurra algo malo. SUSTANTIVO

rural/rural Describe una zona formada por pueblos pequeños y granjas. ADJETIVO

S

sacrifice/sacrificio Algo a lo que renuncias para ayudar a otra persona. SUSTANTIVO

scale/escala Medida de la distancia en un mapa. SUSTANTIVO

scarce/escaso Limitado. ADJETIVO

secondary source/fuente secundaria Algo escrito o hecho por una persona que no fue parte de un suceso ni lo vio ocurrir. SUSTANTIVO

sequence/secuencia El orden en el que ocurren los sucesos. SUSTANTIVO

service/servicio Trabajo que se hace para ayudar a otros. SUSTANTIVO

settle/establecerse Estar en un lugar durante mucho tiempo. VERBO

source/fuente Lugar donde se puede encontrar algo. SUSTANTIVO

suburb/suburbio Comunidad que está cerca de una ciudad. SUSTANTIVO

Supreme Court/Corte Suprema La corte principal de los Estados Unidos. SUSTANTIVO

symbol/símbolo Algo que representa otra cosa. SUSTANTIVO

T

tall tale/cuento exagerado Cuento acerca de una persona con partes que son inventadas y resultan difíciles de creer. SUSTANTIVO

tax/impuesto Dinero que el gobierno cobra a sus ciudadanos. SUSTANTIVO

town/pueblo Comunidad pequeña. SUSTANTIVO

trade/intercambiar Comprar, vender o hacer trueques con bienes y servicios. VERBO

tradition/tradición Algo que se transmite a otros a lo largo del tiempo. SUSTANTIVO

trait/cualidad Algo especial en una persona. SUSTANTIVO

travel/viajar Ir de un lugar a otro. VERBO

treated/tratado Considerado por los demás. VERBO

U

unique/único Que es uno solo y no hay otro igual; especial. ADJETIVO

urban/urbano Describe una gran comunidad formada por una ciudad y los lugares que la rodean. ADJETIVO

V

vaccine/vacuna Producto que protege a las personas y los animales de enfermedades. SUSTANTIVO

veteran/veterano Persona que estuvo en las fuerzas armadas. SUSTANTIVO

volunteer/voluntario Persona que trabaja sin recibir un pago. SUSTANTIVO

vote/votar Tomar una decisión que puede ser contada. VERBO

W

want/deseo Algo que nos gustaría tener pero no necesitamos para poder vivir. SUSTANTIVO

weather/estado del tiempo Lo que ocurre en el aire en un lugar a cierta hora. SUSTANTIVO

Index

This index lists the pages on which topics appear in this book. Page numbers followed by *m* refer to maps. Page numbers followed by *p* refer to photographs. Page numbers followed by *c* refer to charts or graphs. Page numbers followed by *t* refer to timelines. Bold page numbers indicate vocabulary definitions. The terms *See* and *See also* direct the reader to alternate entries.

Credits

Text Acknowledgments

Peachtree Publishers, Ltd.
Good Fortune: My Journey to Gold Mountain by Li Keng Wong. Copyright © by Li Keng Wong. Published by Peachtree Publishers.

Dial Books for Young Readers
My Story by Rosa Parks. Copyright © Rosa Parks. Published by Puffin Books.

Images

Cover
Andy Sacks/Getty Images;

Front Matter
Copyright Page: Rachid Dahnoun/Aurora Open RF/Alamy Stock Photo; i: Andersen Ross/Stockbyte/Getty Images; iii: Camarillo Dr. Albert M.; iii: Dr. James B. Kracht; iii: Dr. Kathy Swan; iii: Dr. Linda B. Bennett; iii: Elfrieda H. Hiebert; iii: Jim Cummins; iii: Kathy Tuchman Glass; iii: Paul Apodaca; iii: Dr. Shirley A. James Hanshaw; iii: Warren J. Blumenfeld; iii: Xiaojian Zhao; XiiiB: Arthur Schatz/The LIFE Picture Collection/Getty Images; xiiiT: Catnap/Alamy Stock Photo; xiv: National Baseball Hall of Fame Library/Major League Baseball Platinum/Getty Images; xix: Catnap/Alamy Stock Photo; xviL: American Stock/ClassicStock/Archive Photos/Getty Images; xviR: Hans Blossey/Alamy Stock Photo

SSH01: Sambr.com/Alamy Stock Photo; SSH02: Sebastien Burel/Shutterstock; SSH04B: NASA; SSH04C: Littleny/Fotolia; SSH04T: Lee Foster/Alamy Stock Photo; SSH05BL: Nasa/Notimex/Newscom; SSH05BR: Jacques Demarthon/AFP/Getty Images; SSH05C: Ansel Adams Publishing Rights Trust/J.Malcolm Greany/Pictures From History/Newscom; SSH05T: Jason Baxter/Alamy Stock Photo; SSH6: Marc Romanelli/Blend Images/Getty Images; SSH7: FatCamera/E+/Getty Images; SSH8: Rich Koele/Shutterstock; CA9B: NetPhotos/Alamy Stock Photo; SSH9T: DNY59/E+/Getty Images; SSH10B: Tetra Images/Alamy Stock Photo; SSH10T: Time Life Pictures/The Life Picture Collection/Getty Images; SSH11CL: Yullika/Shutterstock; SSH11CR: Allan Grant/The Life Picture Collection/Getty Images; SSH11L: Pearson Education, Inc.; SSH11R: DNY59/E+/Getty Images;

Chapter 01
001: Monkey Business Images/Shutterstock; 005: Mike Kemp/Blend Images/Brand X Pictures/Getty Images; 006: David Sacks/DigitalVision/Getty Images; 007: Jay Newman/LWA/Blend Images/Getty Images; 008L: Novastock/Alamy Stock Photo; 008R: Honey & Mehta/Cultura Creative (RF)/Alamy Stock Photo; 009: Hero Images Inc./Alamy Stock Photo; 010: JT Vintage/ Glasshouse Images/Alamy Stock Photo; 011: Chip Somodevilla/Getty Images; 012: Dan Porges/Photolibrary/Getty Images; 013: Image Source/DigitalVision/Getty Images; 018: The Protected Art Archive/Alamy Stock Photo; 019: Sergey Ryzhov/Shutterstock; 020: Library of Congress Prints and Photographs Division[LC-USZ62-61810]; 021: Gabriel Perez/Moment/Getty Images; 024L: Afro Newspaper/Gado/Archive Photos/Getty Images; 024R: Ralph Fiskness/123RF; 025: IS0266MB3/Image Source/Alamy Stock Photo; 028: Jane Tyska/Oakland Tribune/Mct/Newscom; 030B: William Manning/Corbis Documentary/Getty Images; 030T: Stock Montage/Archive Photos/Getty Images; 032: Jan Walters/Alamy Stock Photo

Chapter 02
034: Monkey Business/Fotolia; 046L: David Litman/Shutterstock; 046R: Steven Castro/Shutterstock; 047C: Eric Leslie/Moment/Getty Images; 047L: Skydivecop/Fotolia; 047R: Mariusz S. Jurgielewicz/Shutterstock; 048: HP Canada/Alamy Stock Photo; 049B: Inge Johnsson/Alamy Stock Photo; 049T: Dave Allen Photography/Shutterstock; 052: Kablonk/Golden Pixels LLC/Alamy Stock Photo; 054: Fuse/Corbis/Getty Images; 056: Bettmann/Corbis/Getty Images; 058: American Stock/ClassicStock/Archive Photos/Getty Images; 059: Hans Blossey/Alamy Stock Photo; 060: AE Pictures Inc./DigitalVision/Getty Images; 061: Rolf Schulten/Imagebroker/Alamy Stock Photo; 062: Jeff Smith/Shutterstock; 064: Mark Atkinson/Glow Images; 065: Szefei/Shutterstock; 066B: David R. Frazier/Photolibrary, Inc./Science Source; 066T: Photo Researchers, Inc/Alamy Stock Photo; 068C: Raga Jose Fuste/Prisma Bildagentur AG/Alamy Stock Photo; 068L: Catherine Ledner/The Image Bank/Getty Images; 068R: Bob Kreisel/Alamy Stock Photo; 066: Yato Rurouni/Alamy Stock Photo; 068B: Granger, NYC; 068T: Larry Geddis/Alamy Stock Photo;

Chapter 03
070: Ariel Skelley/Blend Images/Getty Images; 071: Danita Delimont/Gallo Images/Getty Images; 076B: Kuttig - RF - People/Alamy Stock Photo; 076T: Lawrence Migdale/Science Source/Getty Images; 080: Mark R/Shutterstock; 082: Fstockfoto/iStock/Getty Images; 083: Mark Wilson/Getty Images; 084: Bpperry/iStock Editorial/Getty Images; 088: Universal History Archive/Universal Images Group/Getty Images; 095L: Harry Choi/TongRo Images/Alamy Stock Photo; 095R: Bluraz/Fotolia; 096: Handout/Getty Images; 098: Historical/Corbis Historical/Getty Images; 100B: Michael Gottschalk/Photothek/Getty Images; 100T: IanDagnall Computing/Alamy Stock Photo; 103: Novastock/Alamy Stock Photo;

Chapter 04
104: MBI/Stockbroker/Alamy Stock Photo; 110: Dmitry Kalinovsky/Shutterstock; 112B: Mar_d/Shutterstock; 112C: Macrovector/Shutterstock; 112TL: Canon Boy/

Shutterstock; 112TR: Hung Chung Chih/Shutterstock; 113B: Luckypic/Shutterstock; 113T: Nullplus/Getty Images; 114: Radius Images/Alamy Stock Photo; 115: Hero Images Inc./Alamy Stock Photo; 116: Design Pics Inc/Bill & Brigitte Clough/Alamy Stock Photo; 118: H. Armstrong Roberts/ClassicStock/Getty Images; 119: TFoxFoto/Shutterstock; 122: Andrew Olney/OJO Images Ltd/Alamy Stock Photo; 125C: Rudolf MadÃƒÂ¡r/Shutterstock; 125L: Aleksandr Lyadov/Hemera/Getty Images; 125R: Reflex Life/Shutterstock; 126: Jim West/Alamy Stock Photo; 127: Steve Smith Photography/Shutterstock; 128: Catnap/Alamy Stock Photo; 130B: All Canada Photos/Barrett & MacKay/Alamy Stock Photo; 130T: Arthur Schatz/The Life Picture Collection/Getty Images; 132: Doloves/Shutterstock;

Chapter 05

134-135: Rawpixel.com/Fotolia; 138L: Andersen Ross/Blend Images/Getty Images; 139R: ERproductions Ltd/Blend Images/Getty Images; 140B: Danny Moloshok/Alamy Stock Photo; 140T: Anne-Marie Palmer/Alamy Stock Photo; 141: Stocktrek Images, Inc./Alamy Stock Photo; 143: Shutterstock; 144: Chief Sitting Bull(1831-90) 1933(oil on canvas)/Lindneux/Robert Ottokar(1871-1970)/Private Collection/Peter Newark American Pictures/Bridgeman Art Library; 144: Woolaroc Museum Bartlesville, Oklahoma; 145: AFP/Getty Images; 146: Bettmann/Getty Images; 147C: Mike Wintroath/AP Images; 147L: North Wind Picture Archives/Alamy Stock Photo; 147R: Jerry Cooke/Sports Illustrated Classic/Getty Images; 148: AP Images; 149: Diana Walker/Hulton Archive/Getty Images; 150T: Everett Collection Inc/Alamy Stock Photo; 150B: Arthur Schatz/The LIFE Picture Collection/Getty Images; 152: Underwood Archives/Archive Photos/Getty Images; 155: David Cole/Alamy Stock Photo; 155: Everett Historical/Shutterstock; 156L: For Alan/Alamy Stock Photo; 156R: AFP/Getty Images; 157: Fine Art Images/

Heritage Image Partnership Ltd/Alamy Stock Photo; 158B: Alfred Eisenstaedt/The Life Picture Collection/Getty Images; 158T: Bettmann/Getty Images; 159: NARA; 160L: Interfoto/History/Alamy Stock Photo; 160R: 123rf; 162: Jane Addams/Ap Images; 163: Zagalejo; 164: Jim West/Alamy Stock Photo; 165: Bettmann/Getty Images; 166: De Meester Johan/Arterra Picture Library/Alamy Stock Photo; 167: War Posters/Alamy Stock Photo; 170: Wavebreakmedia Ltd PH73/Alamy Stock Photo; 172B: North Wind Picture Archives/Alamy Stock Photo; 172T: Niday Picture Library/Alamy Stock Photo; 173C: AFP/Getty Images; 173L: Diana Walker/Hulton Archive/Getty Images; 173R: Underwood Archives/Archive Photos/Getty Images; 174: Jim West/Alamy Stock Photo;

Chapter 06

176-177: Paul Warner/Getty Images Entertainment/Getty Images; 180: Stu99/iStock Editorial/Getty Images; 181: Theo Wargo/Getty Images Entertainment/Getty Images; 182: Pep Roig/Alamy Stock Photo; 183: Ariel Skelley/Blend Images/Alamy Stock Photo; 184BC: Freebilly/Shutterstock; 184BL: ESB Professional/Shutterstock; 184R: Monkey Business Images Ltd/Getty Images; 184T: Evgenyb/Fotolia; 186-187: Roberto Soncin Gerometta/Lonely Planet Images/Getty Images; 188L: VC-DLH/Prisma/Superstock; 188R: Jenkedco/Shutterstock; 189: Bob Sacha/Corbis Documentary/Getty Images; 190: Xinhua/Alamy Stock Photo; 191: Monkey Business Images/Shutterstock; 197: Library of Congress Prints and Photographs Division [LC-USZ62-56646]; 199: US Navy Photo/Alamy Stock Photo; 200: Piotrek Jastrzebski/Shutterstock; 201: Agence France Presse/Hulton Archive/Getty Images; 202: Corazon Aguirre/Pacific Press/LightRocket/Getty Images; 204: The New York Public Library; 206B: David Madison/Photographer's Choice RF/Getty Images; 206T: National Baseball Hall of Fame Library/Major League Baseball Platinum/Getty Images